Scenic Driving

HAWAII

Richard McMahon

FALCON™

HELENA, MONTANA

A FALCON GUIDE

Falcon Press is continually expanding its list of recreational guidebooks. All books include detailed descriptions, accurate maps, and all the information necessary for enjoyable trips. You can order extra copies of this book and get information and prices for other Falcon guidebooks by writing Falcon Press, P.O. Box 1718, Helena, MT 59624 or calling toll-free 1-800-582-2665. Also, please ask for a free copy of our current catalog. To contact us via e-mail, visit our website at http:\\www.falconguide.com.

Cover photo by Douglas Peebles.
Back cover photo and color section photos by Ann Cecil.
All black and white photos by the author.

Library of Congress Cataloging-in-Publication Data
McMahon, Richard, 1928
    Scenic driving Hawaii / Richard McMahon.
          p. cm.
    ISBN 1-56044-556-4
    1. Hawaii—Tours. 2. Automobile travel—Hawaii—Guidebooks.
I. Title.
DU623.25.M385   1997
919.6904'41—dc21   97-9800
                                          CIP

CAUTION

All participants in the recreational activities suggested by this book must assume the responsibility for their own actions and safety. The information contained in this guidebook cannot replace sound judgement and good decision-making skills, which help reduce risk exposure; nor does this book allow for disclosure of all the potential hazards and risks involved in such activities.

Learn as much as possible about the recreation activities in which you participate, prepare for the unexpected, and be cautious. The reward will be a safer and more enjoyable experience.

 Text pages are printed on recycled paper.

Contents

Acknowledgments

My wife Ann proved to be an invaluable partner in the preparation of this book. She did a fine job drawing the maps for the scenic drives, and chauffeured me hundreds of miles while I reconnoitered and photographed the routes. Orlando Epp read the manuscript and made many useful suggestions. Bob and Tina Owens hosted me several times on the Big Island while the book was in progress. Babs Harrison provided valuable information about Lanai. Without Jackie Johnson Maughan, I never would have started the project, and my editor, Megan Hiller, shepherded it along.

Map legend

Scenic Drive - paved		Interstate	
Scenic Drive - gravel		U. S. Highway	
Scenic Sidetrip - paved		State and County Roads	
Scenic Sidetrip - gravel		Scenic Drive Marker	
Interstate			
Other Roads (paved)		Peak and Elevation	9,782 ft.
Other Roads (gravel)			
City		Lava Flow	
Airport		Crater	
Buildings			
Point of Interest		Cinder Cone	
Campground			
Hiking Trail		Map Orientation	N
River/Creek with Waterfall		Scale of Miles	0 0.5 1 Miles
National/State Park		Scenic Drive Location	PACIFIC OCEAN

Locator Maps

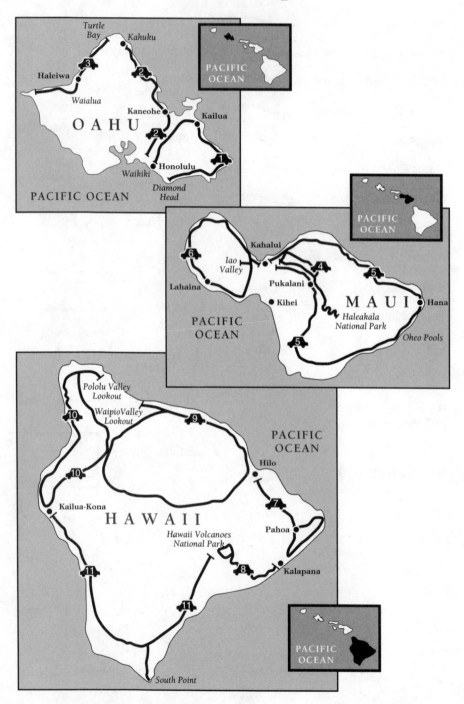

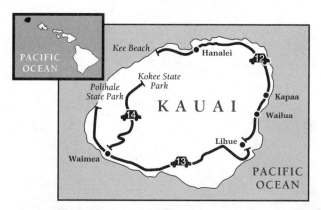

Kee Beach
Hanalei
12
PACIFIC
OCEAN
Kokee State
Park
Polihale
State Park
K A U A I
Kapaa
Wailua
14
Lihue
Waimea
13
PACIFIC
OCEAN

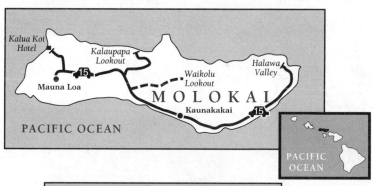

Kalua Koi
Hotel
Kalaupapa
Lookout
Halawa
Valley
15
Waikolu
Lookout
Mauna Loa
M O L O K A I
PACIFIC OCEAN
Kaunakakai
15
PACIFIC
OCEAN

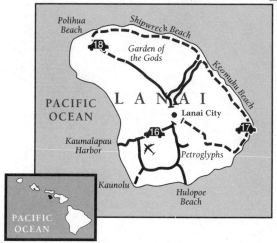

Polihua
Beach
Shipwreck Beach
18
Garden of
the Gods
Keomuku Beach
PACIFIC
OCEAN
L A N A I
Lanai City
16
17
Kaumalapau
Harbor
Petroglyphs
Kaunolu
Hulopoe
Beach
PACIFIC
OCEAN

Le'ie, a native Hawaiian plant, in bloom.

Introduction

Welcome to Hawaii, the 50th state; one of the most beautiful and varied for scenic driving in the country. Justly famous for its beaches and crystal clear ocean, Hawaii offers more diverse regions than perhaps anywhere else in the United States. Lush, tropical rain forests, dry deserts, wave-battered rocky coastlines, alpine mountain slopes, verdant valleys, and a feature found nowhere else in the world—a drive-in, active volcano—all vie for attention in an area smaller than Massachusetts.

Each of the islands of Hawaii has its own charm and special beauty: the beaches and mountains of Oahu, the spectacular Na Pali coast of Kauai, the awesome seacliffs of Molokai, the deep, green valleys of Maui, and the dark, brooding volcanoes of Hawaii all combine to provide an unforgettable experience.

Hawaii is unique in many ways. It is the southernmost point in the United States. It is the only state that was once an independent kingdom, and the only state containing a royal palace. Hawaii has the highest mountain in the world when measured from its base on the ocean floor, and another which is the largest in sheer volume. The tallest seacliffs on earth are found here. The state houses the world's premier astronomic complex, including its largest telescope. Hawaii also has two of the wettest spots on earth and some of the driest. It boasts the world's most active volcano and is the only place in the nation where coffee is grown. Surveys have found Hawaii to be the "healthiest" state in the union and the one where people have the longest life span.

The Hawaiian Islands are the peaks of a submerged volcanic mountain chain, lying at the same latitude as Mexico City and Calcutta. The islands stretch across 1,523 miles of the North Pacific Ocean, from Hawaii in the southeast, to Kure in the northwest. Midway Island, the site of one of the most important battles of World War II, lies within the Hawaiian chain. The islands began forming about 15 million years ago, a mere blink in geological time. But only the uninhabited northwestern islands are that old, and they are little more than atolls today. Of the inhabited islands Kauai is the oldest, at about 6 million years. The state consists of 132 islands, only seven of which are inhabited. The eight largest islands contain over 99.9 percent of the 6,425 square miles of land area. They are, in order of size (largest to smallest), Hawaii, Maui, Oahu, Kauai, Molokai, Lanai, Niihau, and Kahoolawe. The last of these, Kahoolawe, is uninhabited, used until recently as a bombing range by the U.S. military. The island of Hawaii, consisting of 4,034 square miles, is larger than all the other islands combined and contains almost two-thirds of the state's land area. It is the largest island in the United States and is three times the size of the state of Rhode Island. Niihau is privately owned, and no visitors are allowed. It has only 230 inhabitants, almost all of Hawaiian ancestry, who work in ranch operations for the owners. It is the only place in the state where Hawaiian is spoken as the everyday language.

Unlike most of the mainland United States, Hawaii has only two levels of government, state and county. Cities are not separate governmental entities. The state is divided into four counties: Honolulu, Maui, Hawaii, and Kauai. Mayors are county, not city officials. Schools and public libraries are administered by the state, but policing is a county function. In Hawaii, there are no state police.

Hawaii's climate is one of the most pleasant and agreeable anywhere. The average temperature in most of the state ranges between 72°F in the winter to 81°F in the summer. Ocean water temperatures remain between 74° F and 80° F. Although the islands are within the tropics—just south of the Tropic of Cancer—the weather is moderated by the effect of the trade winds. It rains a bit more in the winter months than in summer, but rainfall in Hawaii is more a matter of location than season, and it varies greatly over the state. The average annual rainfall in Honolulu is 24 inches, in Lahaina it is 14, in Hana 69; and in Hilo, a heavy 141. Generally speaking, the windward sides of all islands receive considerably more rain than their leeward sides, and coastal areas receive less than inland regions. Much of the rain comes at night, or in the early morning hours, with the remainder of the day often clear and bright.

Although Captain James Cook is credited with discovering Hawaii in 1778, it was actually the Polynesians who found the islands more than a thousand years before Cook's arrival. Setting out in large, double-hulled sailing canoes, probably from the Marquesas, and guided only by stars, winds, currents, and clouds, these courageous seafarers crossed over two thousand miles of unknown ocean to settle the Hawaiian Islands. Little is known of the period between their arrival and Cook's discovery. The Hawaiians had no written language and they relied on oral chants passed from one generation to the next to record their history, making it difficult to separate legend from fact.

Shortly after Cook's visit, Kamehameha, a young chieftain from the island of Hawaii, began a campaign of conquest to bring all the islands of the chain under his rule. Assisted by Western advisers and their technology, including cannon and warships, he subdued all the islands but Kauai, which he later brought under his control through negotiation. In 1810, for the first time, all the Hawaiian Islands were united under one ruler.

In 1820 a group of New England missionaries arrived in the islands and gradually converted most of the Hawaiian people to Christianity. Over the years, the influence of the missionaries and their descendants resulted in increasing American social, political, and economic

Pineapple fields in central Oahu.

control. The Hawaiian kingdom continued as an independent nation under the successors of Kamehameha until 1893, when it was overthrown by a coup, headed primarily by influential American businessmen. The leaders of the coup were interested in bringing Hawaii under the American flag to receive favorable treatment for Hawaiian sugar imported into the United States. At first, the U.S. government did not look favorably upon the overthrow of the Hawaiian monarchy. But the Spanish-American War changed American perspectives in the Pacific; when the Philippines became a U.S. territory, Hawaii's strategic location became obvious, and in 1898 the former island kingdom was annexed by the United States. Administered as a territory for 61 years, Hawaii became the 50th state of the union on August 21, 1959.

Driving in Hawaii is no different than anywhere else in the country, except in getting there. The roads are excellent, well laid out, and there are even three *interstate* highways (designated as such because of the source of their funding, not because they connect to another state). Other than cargo barge traffic, there is no sea transportation between the islands except for a partially subsidized passenger ferry running between Kaunakakai on Molokai and Lahaina, Maui, used primarily to bring workers on Molokai to hotel industry jobs on Maui. Travel between islands is by air. Hawaiian, Aloha, and Mahalo Airlines provide frequent, fast service to all main airports, and several commuter airlines fly to the smaller airfields.

Rental car agencies have offices on every island. Prices are fairly reasonable, except on Molokai and Lanai, where lower demand results in higher operational costs. A four percent excise tax and a two dollars per day state tax are added to the rental fee. Although the supply of vehicles is relatively large, it is important to have confirmed reservations, especially during weekends and holidays. It is not unusual for someone to deplane at a neighbor island terminal and find every car rental agency sold out. Some rental companies place restrictions on the use of certain routes, such as the Saddle Road on the island of Hawaii. These are often unreasonable and arbitrary and have more to do with the cost of recovery of the vehicle from a remote area than with the condition or safety of the road. Many drivers shop for companies without the restrictions. Four-wheel-drive vehicles are available on all islands, but care must be taken to ensure that the vehicle is what it is supposed to be. Some rental companies disconnect the four-wheel-drive train.

It is possible to ship cars from island to island, although for the average tourist it is not economical to do so. However, for a long-term visitor, who has purchased a car or small recreational vehicle (RV) in Hawaii and intends to spend a considerable amount of time on another island, this may be a viable option. Young Brothers provides barge service to all islands, and the cost of shipping a vehicle up to the size of a Volkswagen (VW) van is $160 one way, or $265 round-trip if accomplished within thirty days. It is no longer possible to rent any type of camper or recreational vehicle in Hawaii, and although there are good campgrounds on all islands, there are no hookups for RVs. Some residents use small RVs in campgrounds (VW poptops, pickup truck campers), but in most cases these vehicles are restricted to the parking lots.

All campgrounds mentioned in this book require permits, except the drive-in campgrounds in the national parks. Campgrounds are identified as coming under county, state, federal, or private jurisdiction, and addresses or phone numbers for acquiring permits are given in the Appendix. As is the case almost anywhere, facilities vary considerably. Those planning to do much camping may find it useful to refer to *Camping Hawaii,* published by the University of Hawaii Press, which lists and fully describes more than 120 campgrounds and low-cost cabins throughout the state.

Do not leave anything of value in a parked car, whether in the locked passenger section or the trunk. Thefts of property from vehicles are on the rise in Hawaii, particularly from rental cars, which are easily identified. Car thieves on all islands are adept at breaking into vehicles in a matter of seconds.

All of the scenic drives described in this book can be completed in one day. Some of them, however, such as the trip to Hana and around Maui's south coast, are worth an overnight or longer stay. When this is the case, it is noted in the drive description. Due to Hawaii's benign climate, all of the drives may be enjoyed at any time of the year.

A glossary of Hawaiian words used in this book appears at the end of the scenic drive descriptions. It is not a list of all the Hawaiian words you might find useful, but rather those that will make this book more understandable and your scenic drives more enjoyable.

Waikiki Beach, with Diamond Head in the center.

The scenic drives described were meant to be driven with this book in hand. While the maps in the book are all you will need to find your way and enjoy the sights along the drive, a good road map will help you understand the drive in relation to other parts of the islands. The American Automobile Association (AAA) publishes a good map showing all the islands that it makes available free to its members. Similar maps are available for sale in Hawaii's bookstores, newsstands, supermarkets, and department stores. More detailed, individual maps of each island are published by the University of Hawaii Press (Molokai and Lanai are on one map) and can be purchased as above or ordered directly from the press at 2840 Kolowalu Street, Honolulu, HI 96822, phone, 808-956-8255. Cost of each map at the time of this publication was $2.95.

For those interested in reading more about the Hawaiian Islands, either before or during your stay, the following books are a good starting point.

Shoal of Time, by Gavan Daws. University of Hawaii Press, Honolulu, 1974. One of the best histories of the Hawaiian Islands, told in a relaxed, readable style.

A Hawaiian Reader, edited by Day and Stroven. Mutual Publishing, Honolulu, 1984. Selections by thirty authors writing about Hawaii, to include Robert Louis Stevenson, Mark Twain, and Jack London.

Myths and Legends of Hawaii, by W. D. Westervelt, selected and edited by A. Grove Day. Mutual Publishing, Honolulu, 1987. An abridged, pocket size version of a definitive work.

Molokai, by O. A. Bushnell. University of Hawaii Press, Honolulu, 1975. A fictional, but accurate account of the conditions in the early days of the leper colony at Kalaupapa.

Adventuring in Hawaii, by Richard McMahon. Sierra Club Books, 1996. A guide for those who would like to do more than drive and sunbathe, this books covers such activities as hiking, backpacking, scuba, snorkeling, surfing, kayaking, and more.

OAHU

Oahu, the third largest of the islands, supports eighty-one percent of the state's population, plus up to 100,000 tourists on any given day. Its most popular tourist destination is Waikiki. Honolulu is the capital of the state and its largest city. Oahu came late to its pre-eminent position. For hundreds of years the seat of power and population was the Big Island of Hawaii, giving way to Maui for a short period in the mid-nineteenth century. Not until the development of Honolulu Harbor, and later Pearl Harbor, did Oahu come to the fore.

Oahu was formed from two volcanoes, the Waianae and the Koolau, their lava flows joining together to form the island's central plain. Geologists estimate that Oahu is between 2.2 and 3.4 million years old. Unlike most mainland locations, the City and County of Honolulu form one governmental entity with jurisdiction over the entire island of Oahu.

Despite all the hotels, office buildings, freeways, and other man-made clutter, Oahu easily holds its own with the other islands when it comes to sheer natural beauty. The fluted cliffs of the Koolau Pali drape the mountains behind Kailua and Kaneohe like a giant, green theater curtain. The mirror-still waters of Kaneohe Bay reflect the beauty of the hills and the shoreline as perfectly as a Tahitian lagoon. Oahu's deep valleys, many ending at waterfalls and plunge pools, are as verdant and mysterious as those on any remote South Seas island. And far from Waikiki, miles of isolated, empty beaches rarely show a footprint in the sand. Some of the most scenic drives in Hawaii are found here.

Area: 594 square miles
Population: 840,000
Airport: Honolulu.
Rental car offices: airport, Honolulu, Waikiki, Kaneohe, and most military bases.

1

The Nuuanu Pali, Makapuu Cliffs, and the Southeast Shore

General description: This 36-mile drive crosses the Koolau Mountains on the scenic Pali Highway, descends to the windward shore of Oahu, and turns south, with the shoreline on the left and the sheer cliffs of the Koolau on the right. Rounding Makapuu Point and passing Sandy Beach, the drive closely follows the rocky, wave-pounded shoreline to Hanauma Bay and then returns to Honolulu through the suburbs of Hawaii Kai. Ten beach parks line the route, and beautiful, long white sand beaches fringe Kailua and Waimanalo Bays.

Special attractions: Nuuanu Pali Lookout, Sea Life Park, Makapuu Point, Koko Crater, Halona Blowhole, Hanauma Bay, hiking, camping, swimming, boating, surfing, sailboarding, body surfing, snorkeling, scuba diving.

Location: The southeast portion of the island of Oahu.

Drive route numbers: Hawaii Highway 61 (Pali Highway), Nuuanu Pali Drive, Hawaii Highway 72 (Kalanianaole Highway).

Camping: Four campgrounds are available along the route: Bellows Beach (weekends only), Waimanalo Bay, Waimanalo Beach, and Makapuu Beach, all of them county parks. Permits are required.

Services: Kailua: All services except accommodations (some bed-and-breakfasts available). Waimanalo: Gas, limited shopping, some small restaurants. Gas, shopping, and restaurants are available along the route after Hanauma Bay.

Nearby attractions: Hoomaluhia Botanical Garden, *Ulu Po Heiau,* Kailua Beach, Makapuu Lighthouse, Makapuu tide pools, Koko Crater Botanical Garden, Diamond Head Summit Trail.

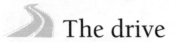 ## The drive

The drive begins by turning north at the Pali Highway (HI 61) from Vineyard Boulevard in downtown Honolulu, or by exiting at Pali Highway (north) from the westbound lane of the H-1 Freeway. After about 2.5 miles, the route turns to the right onto Nuuanu Pali Drive. Here, a tropical rain forest virtually engulfs the road. Giant philodendron vines climb the tree trunks, and the trees themselves join above the road to close off the sky. Small waterfalls send their streams winding through lush vegetation into half-hidden ponds and the few houses seem suspended in the trees.

The Nuuanu Pali, Makapuu Cliffs, and the Southeast Shore

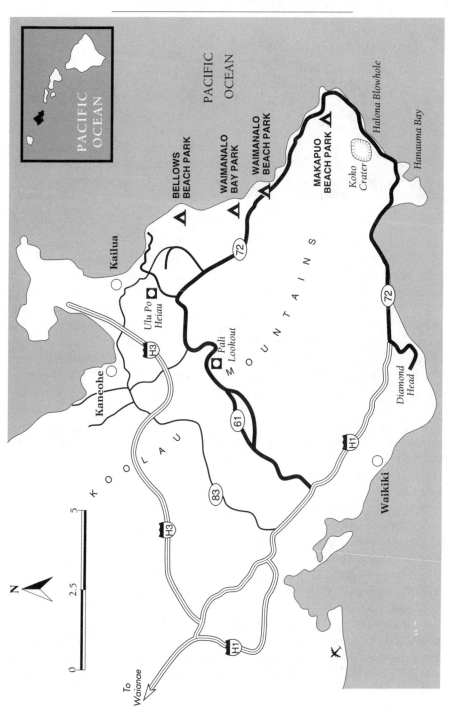

Olomana from the Pali Highway (HI 61).

The route rejoins HI 61 and soon reaches the Nuuanu Pali Lookout with its sweeping view of windward Oahu. In 1795 Kamehameha, soon to be the first king of all the Hawaiian Islands, landed his forces on Oahu in a war to bring the island under his rule. During a long battle, his warriors gradually forced the Oahu army back to the headwall of Nuuanu Valley, where many of the Oahu warriors were pushed over the cliff to their deaths on the rocks below. During the construction of the first improved road over the Pali, between 1882 and 1897, about eight hundred skulls and other bones were found at the base of the precipice. They have been attributed to the hapless Oahu defenders.

Another feature of the battle are the two notches in the ridgeline visible above HI 61 (when you are driving from Honolulu) on the right side of the road. These notches were constructed on order of *Kalanikupule*, the Oahu chief, as emplacements for two cannons. These weapons virtually stopped Kamehameha's advance until he sent a party of warriors to outflank the position over a dangerous route along the knife-edged ridgeline to the east.

The Old Pali Road, still visible and accessible from the lookout, served as the connection to windward Oahu for fifty-five years, until the present road with its two tunnels was opened in 1957. Three years later, the Likelike Highway provided a second route to the windward side. Although somewhat overgrown by vegetation, the old road makes a good scenic route for a hike or a short stroll.

From the lookout, the drive returns to HI 61 and drops steeply to windward via a long hairpin turn, the green cliffs and blue ocean vying for attention. Just short of 4 miles past the lookout, the scenic route turns right off HI 61 and onto HI 72. However, a short excursion straight ahead on HI

Waimanalo Beach, three miles of white sand and blue sea.

61 allows a visit to *Ulu Po Heiau* on the left side of the road at the edge of the Kawainui Marsh, a former fishpond. *Ulu Po* was a *luakini,* meaning that human sacrifices were offered here, and it may also have served as an agricultural *heiau* (temple). It was constructed in A.D. 400, only a few years after the earliest confirmed cultural deposits for Oahu, found at Bellows Beach, which date to A.D. 323.

This diversion from the drive may also include a visit to Kailua Beach, one of the finest white sand swimming beaches on the island, and a well-known sailboarding location. To reach the beach, continue on HI 61, veer right on Kailua Road, and follow it to the beach. Kayaks can be rented at the beach for excursions to the Moku Lua, two prominent islands about 0.75 mile offshore. The return to the drive can either be by backtracking to HI 72 (a **left** turn this time), or by driving through the town of Kailua (population 36,000), a major suburb of Honolulu.

Three miles from the HI 61/72 junction is the town of Waimanalo (population 3,500), once the center of a large sugar plantation. Sugar operations ceased in the 1940s, and little farming is done now except for small plots of bananas, papayas, plant nurseries, and a pig farm. Most of these activities are not visible from the road. The scenic route reaches the shoreline at Waimanalo Beach, 4.5 miles of lovely sandy shoreline, lapped by gentle waves, fringed by ironwood trees, and backed by the sheer walls of the Koolau Pali. Three campgrounds are located nearby: Bellows Beach,

Waimanalo Bay, and Waimanalo Beach, all relatively close together. The best of these is Waimanalo Bay.

Once past Waimanalo, there is little habitation along the route until the other side of Hanauma Bay. Manana Island, the high rocky islet offshore, is better known as Rabbit Island, because rabbits were once introduced there as a business venture. Today, the rabbits are gone, and the island is a bird sanctuary.

Television buffs might be interested to know that one of the homes on the beach side of the road (well protected from view) is the mansion that Tom Selleck as *Magnum, P. I.* shared with his landlord, Higgins (John Hillerman).

Makapuu Beach Park, a dramatic setting at the base of the black Makapuu cliffs, is one of the most popular body surfing beaches on Oahu. Hang gliders sometimes launch from the cliffs high above the beach, soaring over the sea to eventually land near the park. A campground is located here. From the beach park the road climbs to Makapuu Point, where, at a small pullout, a look back at the road reveals a magnificent seascape, a long windward coast panorama of green mountains and blue sea and sky.

Rounding the point, HI 72 turns sharply south, temporarily leaving the coast. Less than 0.5 mile farther, a paved road (closed to motorized vehicles) makes a great 2-mile round trip hike to a lookout overlooking the

Highway 72 winds along Oahu's rocky south shore.

Makapuu Lighthouse. The view is much more expansive than the one from the highway. Also from this road, a rocky path descends to the Makapuu tide pools, a series of small pools carved in the reef, where blowholes make a great show during high seas.

The drive returns to the coast at Sandy Beach, another body surfing favorite, and Koko Crater looms to the front. An attractive botanical garden, specializing in cactus and succulents, is located inside the crater. About 2.5 miles past the Makapuu Lookout, a turnoff to the left leads to Halona Blowhole, where incoming swells force water through a narrow hole in the reef, sending sprays skyward with a roar. Additional turnouts are located at Lanai and Molokai Lookouts, and on clear days those islands are visible across the Kaiwi Channel.

Hanauma Bay, Hawaii's most famous snorkeling spot, is 2.3 miles past the blowhole. Created when one side of a shoreline crater eroded to let in the sea, the almost circular bay frames one of the most beautiful beaches found anywhere. Unfortunately, its popularity brings large crowds, and parking is difficult. Hanauma is best visited early in the morning before the crowds arrive.

Leaving the bay, HI 72 returns to Honolulu along Maunalua Bay, through the suburbs of Hawaii Kai and Aina Haina, passing attractive beach parks. The bay is popular with boaters and scuba divers. Near the end of the trip, a

Honolulu from the bunker atop Diamond Head.

worthwhile side trip is the short hike to the peak of Diamond Head. An easy trail from inside its crater leads through tunnels and staircases to a former military bunker on top, providing good views of the city and the coastline. To reach the crater, turn left off HI 72 at Kilauea Avenue, at the beginning of the H-1 Freeway. Proceed about 1.3 miles to 18th Avenue. Turn left again, continue for 0.5 mile to the intersection with Diamond Head Road. A right turn leads to an almost immediate left into the tunnel leading into the crater. Parking is available at the trailhead.

2
The Windward Coast:
Green Hills and Blue Sea

General description: This 40-mile drive, with the Koolau Mountains on one side and the blue Pacific on the other, follows the beautiful windward coast of Oahu from the spectacular Koolau Pali above Kaneohe, north to the former sugar-producing town of Kahuku.

Special attractions: Koolau Pali, Kaneohe Bay, Heeia State Park, Kualoa Regional Park, Chinaman's Hat Island, Crouching Lion, Kahana Bay, Kahana Valley State Park, Polynesian Cultural Center, Laie Point, Mormon Temple, Kahuku Sugar Mill, hiking, camping, swimming, boating, fishing.

Location: The northeast shore of the island of Oahu.

Drive route numbers: Hawaii Highways 83 and 836, accessed from Hawaii Highway 63 (Likelike Highway).

Camping: There are seven oceanside campgrounds and one forest campground along the route. Six of these, Hoomaluhia Botanical Garden, and Kualoa, Swanzy, Kahana Bay, Hauula, and Kokololio Beach Parks, are under county jurisdiction. Two campgrounds, Malaekahana State Recreation Area and Kahuku Section-Malaekahana, are under state jurisdiction. Permits are required.

Services: Kaneohe: All services except accommodations. Gas, food, and limited shopping are available in some of the small towns along the route. Accommodations at Rodeway Motel in Laie, 808-293-9282; and Turtle Bay Hilton Hotel, 808-293-8811, three miles north of Kahuku. Some vacation rentals and bed-and-breakfasts can be found along the route.

Nearby attractions: Hoomaluhia Botanical Garden, Kailua Beach, Senator Fong's Plantation and Gardens, Sacred Falls, Laie Point, Kahuku Point, Waimea Falls Park, north shore surfing and swimming beaches.

 The drive

The spectacular *pali* (cliffs) of the Koolau Mountains, verdant valleys, and beautiful beaches and bays, make this drive one of the most scenic in the islands. Eleven beach parks line the route. Once past the town of Kaneohe, the road enters rural Oahu. Few tourist attractions can be found, except for the beauty of the landscape. In the late 1700s, Kamehameha rewarded his chiefs with the isolated lands on the windward side of the mountains after

The Windward Coast:
Green Hills and Blue Sea

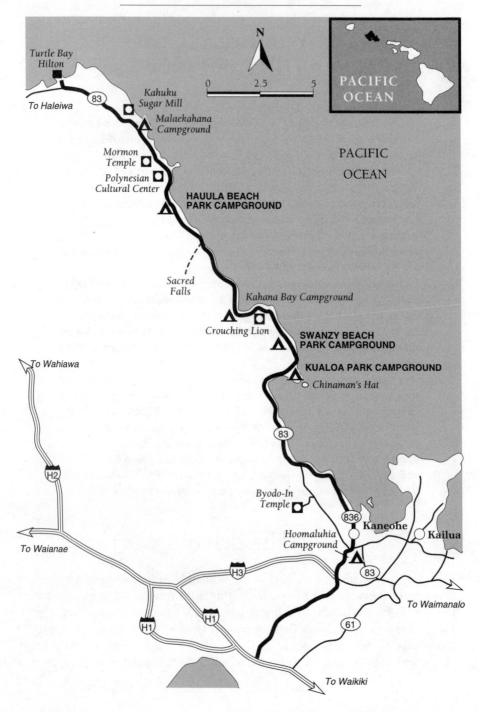

N

0   2.5   5

PACIFIC
OCEAN

Turtle Bay
Hilton

To Haleiwa

83

Kahuku
Sugar Mill

Malaekahana
Campground

Mormon
Temple

Polynesian
Cultural Center

PACIFIC

OCEAN

**HAUULA BEACH
PARK CAMPGROUND**

Sacred
Falls

Kahana Bay Campground

Crouching Lion

**SWANZY BEACH
PARK CAMPGROUND**

To Wahiawa

KUALOA PARK CAMPGROUND

Chinaman's Hat

83

H2

Byodo-In
Temple

836   **Kaneohe**   **Kailua**

Hoomaluhia
Campground

To Waianae

H3

83

To Waimanalo

H1   H1

61

To Waikiki

his conquest of Oahu. Fanned by the northeast trade winds and watered by streams rushing from the mountains, the district is characterized by lush valleys and fertile plains. But it was not until 1957, when a modern road was completed across the Koolau from Nuuanu Valley, that significant development and population growth began.

Sugar was the first major commercial crop to be planted on the windward side, and waving fields of cane once stretched from Waimanalo to Kahuku. When the invention of artesian wells made it cheaper to grow the cane on the leeward side, sugar production waned, was replaced by rice, and then pineapple. Cattle grazing eventually took over much of the windward farmland. Today, all three crops are gone, but some cattle still graze the outlying areas. Farming on the windward side is now limited to smaller plots, devoted mainly to bananas, papaya, assorted vegetables, and ornamental plants.

Although it receives more rain than other regions of Oahu, the weather along the route is mostly excellent. Clouds sometimes cover the Koolau summit, while leaving the coastal area sunny and clear. Rain showers often come and go quickly, providing frequent rainbows.

Access to the drive from Honolulu is via the Likelike Highway, HI 63, which begins from the H-1 Freeway in Honolulu. Leaving the H-1, HI 63 passes through Kalihi Valley, with steep ridges lining both its sides. The

Windward Oahu from the Likelike Highway (HI 63). Pointed mountain in the center foreground is Olomana.

upper part of the valley is home to Oahu's most unusual wild animal. In 1916 a pair of Australian rock wallabies escaped from a circus and established a small population in the uppermost reaches of the valley. Although several outdoor-oriented groups organize occasional "wallaby watch" hikes, the animals are rarely seen.

Eight miles from the freeway, HI 63 crosses the Koolau Mountains via the Wilson Tunnel, exiting suddenly to a sweeping view of the windward coast. The route bears immediately left, where the Koolau Pali soars at its closest and most awe-inspiring. It is as though a giant theater curtain had descended from the sky, its green folds plunging over 2,000 feet to the highway and the plain below. HI 63 drops quickly to the town of Kaneohe, passing under the viaduct of the H-3 Freeway, and reaching an intersection with Kamehameha Highway, HI 836. The drive turns left on HI 836, leading through the center of Kaneohe town.

Kaneohe (population 35,000) has attractive neighborhoods along the shoreline and close to the mountains, but its center is a traffic-congested collection of shopping and business enterprises, including two malls. Hoomaluhia Botanical Garden, occupying a dramatic location at the foot of the Koolau Pali, contains 400 acres of plants and trees from various tropical areas, hiking trails, a small lake, and uncrowded camping in one of the most serene and spacious sites found anywhere. All facilities are new and mod-

Catamaran leaving Heeia Pier in Kaneohe Bay.

Peaceful Kaneohe Bay, the only true lagoon in the Hawaiian Islands, with mountains and Chinaman's Hat Island in the distance.

ern. It is open daily except Christmas and New Year's Day, and entry is free. Enter from Luluku Road.

Leaving Kaneohe, the route follows the coast along beautiful Kaneohe Bay, for the next 10 miles. Heeia State Park, about 1.3 miles north of Kaneohe, provides a good view of Heeia Fishpond, one of the best examples of an ancient Hawaiian fishpond in the state. Its basic structure is still intact. Fishponds were constructed to store fish alive until needed. One or more gateways to the sea could be opened to allow fish to enter, and closed to keep them in the pond. Most of the ponds were owned or controlled by the chiefs or other members of the *alii* (nobility).

Just past Heeia State Park, at Heeia Kea Pier, a glass bottom boat makes tours of the coral reefs of the bay. A little over 2 miles from the pier, HI 836 intersects HI 83 (Kamehameha Highway), which now becomes the scenic route for the remainder of the drive. Turn right (north) here. However, before doing so, a side trip is possible, to the Byodo-In Temple—a replica of an 11th century Buddhist temple in Kyoto, Japan. It is located 1.7 miles south of the HI 836/83 intersection in a lovely, serene setting in the Valley of the Temples Cemetery. Admission is charged.

Continuing north, a short distance from the HI 836/83 intersection, Senator Fong's Plantation and Gardens displays a large variety of tropical trees and plants on over 700 carefully tended acres. A tram, accessible via

Camping is permitted at Kualoa Regional Park, one of the prettiest settings on Oahu.

Pulama Road, takes visitors through the park-like setting. There is an admission fee.

Beyond Fong's plantation, some of the most striking mountain scenery in all the islands now unfolds on the left side of the road. Deeply incised valleys, guarded by sheer, knife-like ridges, proclaim the virtually inaccessible nature of the region. Hikers have lost their lives here, or simply disappeared trying to prove otherwise.

Kualoa Regional Park, about 5 miles from Fong's, is situated in one of the most sacred places of ancient Hawaii, and is on the National Register of Historic Sites. Four *heiau* were known to have existed here, and many high-ranking Hawaiian chiefs made the area their home. A place of refuge was located here, and Kualoa was the seat of Lono, the god of harvests. In 1976, a replica of an ancient Hawaiian double-hulled sailing canoe, *Hokulea*, sailed from Hawaii to Tahiti without instrumentation, navigating by using only ocean swells, currents, and stars. Upon its return, Kualoa was chosen as the place for its ceremonial landing.

Two campgrounds are located in the park, the more secluded of the two reserved for groups (a family "group" qualifies). Molii, one of the few still functioning fish ponds in Hawaii, can be seen by walking south and then west along the beach in the park. Mullet, milkfish, and threadfish are raised in the pond.

Mokolii Island, also known as Chinaman's Hat, stands prominently 0.25 mile offshore. The island is said to have been created by *Hiaka*, the sister of *Pele*, when she killed a dragon and set its flukes upright in the sea as a landmark. At low tide it is possible to wade to the island, where a rough trail leads to its peak. Wearing old tennis shoes or other footgear is advisable, due to the broken coral on the sea bottom. Non-swimmers should be aware of holes and crevices in the sea floor where depths change without warning.

From Kualoa to Kahana Bay the dramatic cliffs of the Koolau reach their closest point to the road. Sheer walls 1,500 feet high drop almost to the highway, barring entry to the Koolau rain forests. Five miles from Kualoa, Swanzy Beach County Park offers camping on weekends only. Just ahead is the Crouching Lion Restaurant, named for the lion-like rock formation that sits above the road. To Hawaiians, who had never seen a lion, this figure was *Kauhiimakaokalani*, the shape changer, posing as a dog.

Around the curve lies Kahana Bay, with its tree-lined, crescent beach and rugged mountain backdrop. At low tide, just before rounding the bay, Huilua Fishpond is visible off the road to the right. Kahana offers an attractive campground, located in the tree line fronting the beach. Behind the bay, in Kahana Valley State Park, a trail system winds through a tropical forest, visiting two secluded pools.

Three miles past Kahana, Sacred Falls State Park offers a 5-mile round-

Entrance to the Polynesian Cultural Center in Laie.

trip walk along a stream to a lovely waterfall and pool. It is typical of many such lovely pools throughout the islands, most of which are much harder to reach. According to Hawaiian legend, the 80-foot high falls and its pool are sacred to *Kamapuaa* the demigod, half man and half pig, who was the lover of *Pele*, goddess of fire. Do not make this trip if it is raining; the trail is subject to flash floods, and people have lost their lives here.

The Polynesian Cultural Center, in the town of Laie (population 5,500), is one of Oahu's most popular tourist attractions. Full-size replicas of seven different Polynesian villages occupy its 72 acres, and interpretive guides acquaint visitors with the culture and traditions of each. A Pageant of Canoes, a luau, and an evening Polynesian show are also offered. A full afternoon and part of an evening are needed to see everything. Laie Point, a wave-battered rocky promontory, can be reached by making a right turn at the Laie Shopping Center, and driving about 0.5 mile.

Brigham Young University's Hawaii Campus and the Mormon Temple lie left of the road, just past the shopping center. Mormons first settled this area in 1864. Although the university is open to all, it specializes in offering an education to young people from the Pacific area. Half a mile north of town, Malaekahana State Recreation Area's beautiful and virtually empty beach hosts two excellent campgrounds. Another wade-to island offshore is a bird sanctuary, and although walking along its perimeter beach is permitted, walking inland is not allowed.

Two miles north of Laie, the small, quiet town of Kahuku marks the end of this scenic drive. Once the center of a sugar plantation, many of its 3,000 residents are retired sugar workers. Plagued by salt winds, and with vital sunshine restricted by the mountains, the plantation was never as profitable as others on Oahu and finally closed in 1971. The old sugar mill has been refurbished as a tourist attraction, with a restaurant, snack bar, and several shops. A large aquaculture venture north of the town once produced prawns and shrimp on the former sugar acreage. After operating for several years, it did not prove to be economically viable and was forced to close. Although much of the former cane land now lies fallow, papaya, bananas, and other tropical crops have taken over from sugar, and Kahuku corn has a reputation in the islands for a special sweetness and flavor.

3
The North Shore: Sand and Surf

General description: This 20-mile coastal drive begins at Turtle Bay on the northeastern tip of Oahu and follows the north shore to the end of the road near the northwestern tip of the island.

Special attractions: Turtle Bay, Sunset Beach, *Puu o Mahuka Heiau*, Waimea Bay, *Hale o Lono Heiau*, Waimea Falls Park, hiking, camping, swimming, snorkeling, scuba, surfing, sailboarding, boating, fishing, beachcombing, parachute jumping, glider rides.

Location: The North Shore of the island of Oahu.

Drive route numbers:Hawaii Highways 83 (Kamehameha Highway) and 930 (Farrington Highway).

Camping: Two public campgrounds, Kaiaka Bay and Mokuleia County Beach Parks (permits required), and two private campgrounds, Camp Mokuleia and Camp Erdman, are located along the route.

Services: Haleiwa: gas, restaurants, shopping. Waialua: gas, limited shopping. The only hotel is the Turtle Bay Hilton, at the beginning of the drive. Some bed-and-breakfasts and vacation rentals are located along the route.

Nearby attractions: Kaena Point Natural Area Reserve, Kahuku Point, Kahuku Sugar Mill, Mormon Temple, Polynesian Cultural Center, Sacred Falls.

 The drive

The North Shore of Oahu is a world-famous surfing destination. Some authorities call it the Aspen of surfing. But while Aspen has developed tastefully to accommodate skiers, the North Shore remains mostly undeveloped and somewhat seedy. It is essentially a one-road-wide community, and residents seem to want it to stay that way. Honolulu County has cooperated by directing development toward other parts of the island. Despite pockets of run-down housing and rickety store fronts, the combination of rural, mountain, and ocean scenery make the drive interesting as well as beautiful.

This oceanfront route includes spectacular coastal scenery, distant mountain views, and many of the most famous surfing and swimming beaches in the Hawaiian Islands. Nine beach parks are located along the route, plus miles of undeveloped sandy beach shoreline. Although homes line the road along most of the eastern portion of the drive, only two small

Scuba divers entering the water at Shark's Cove.

towns lie on the route, Haleiwa and Waialua. Mount Kaala, the highest point on Oahu at 4,020 feet, dominates much of the drive. Huge waves batter this coast in winter, attracting surfers from around the world anxious to test their skills, and tourists eager to watch them.

A railroad once paralleled this route, beginning in Honolulu, running along Oahu's western shore, rounding the island at Kaena Point, and ending in Kahuku. Although it carried passengers, its main function was to transport sugar from the northern plantations to Honolulu. Military requirements of World War II brought construction of roads through central Oahu, and after the war it became cheaper and quicker to transport the sugar by road. The railroad finally ceased operation at the end of 1947.

The drive begins at the entrance to the Turtle Bay Hilton Hotel, near Kahuku Point, the northernmost tip of Oahu. Turtle Bay, accessible from the hotel grounds, is a pretty crescent of sand west of the hotel. A mile-long beach hike leads east from the hotel grounds to Kahuku Point, a wild, isolated place.

Driving southwest from the hotel on HI 83, a line of windmills comes into view on the hills to the left. Designed to provide wind-generated power to augment Oahu's electric grid, the project is still functioning, but has been plagued with technical problems. The largest wind generator in the world is located here, its 100 meter blade longer than a football field. It may be glimpsed by looking backward from the route on the mountain side of the road.

The North Shore: Sand and Surf

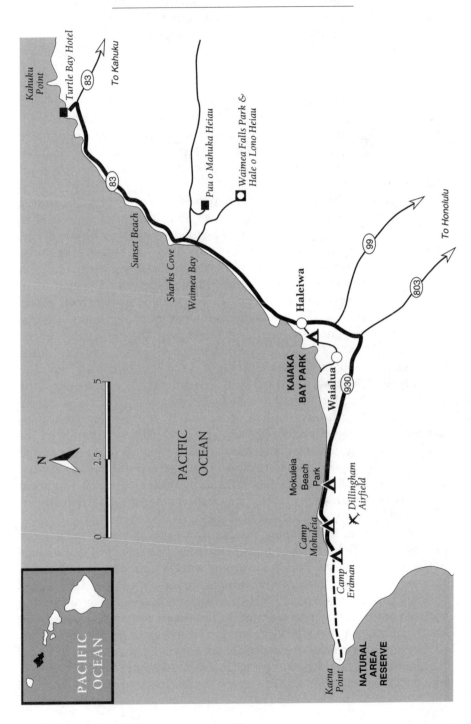

An interesting historical footnote involves these same hills. On December 7, 1941, a two-man radar site just above the highway picked up the Japanese planes on their way to attack Pearl Harbor. They reported the planes to their duty officer, who assumed they were a flight of U.S. B-17 bombers due to arrive from the mainland that same day, and told them to forget about it!

About 3.5 miles from the hotel, Sunset Beach appears on the right, off the highway. For a world-famous surfing site, there are, surprisingly, no facilities. Parking is along the shoulder of the road; it is crowded and difficult, and tour buses add to the problem. The only restrooms are portable toilets, and there are no showers and no water. But the beach is beautiful, with deep, white sand and great views. Swimming can be dangerous, especially in winter.

From Sunset westward, the route passes more world-famous surfing sites—Gas Chambers, Banzai Pipeline, and Chun's Reef, to name a few. Most are not visible from the highway, but are announced by cars with empty surf racks parked along the road. Shark's Cove, two miles from Sunset, is a popular snorkeling and dive spot. Old-time residents say the cove got its name from a large tiger shark that once frequented the area. However, the increase in human activity over the years has apparently driven the shark to more peaceful waters. Although calm in summer, winter swells bring waves crashing into the cove and a neighboring tide pool, sending spray as high as 30 feet.

Just past Shark's Cove, at the Foodland supermarket, the drive turns left off HI 83 onto Pupukea Road, for a visit to the *Puu O Mahuka Heiau*. The access road to the *heiau* is marked by a sign on the right, near the top of the ridge and behind the store. *Puu O Mahuka* was a *luakini heiau*—a temple where human sacrifices were performed. In 1794, three sailors from Captain George Vancouver's ship *Daedalus* were reportedly sacrificed here. Today, the *heiau* is little more than a pile of rock, but the view of the coastline all the way to Kaena Point is unsurpassed. At the end of Pupukea Road, a dirt road leads to the Kaunala Trail, a 5-mile hiking loop through a beautiful coastal forest. Because it lies within a military training area, the trail is open for hiking only on weekends and holidays.

Returning to HI 83, a few hundred yards past the Foodland store is Three Tables, which gets its name from three flat patches of reef that rise out of the sea just offshore. This is a maritime conservation district with excellent snorkeling and scuba diving. Turning around a bend, the drive circles Waimea Bay, where waves 25 feet and higher thunder ashore during the winter months. Traffic halts to watch the few expert surfers who brave these winter monsters. Paradoxically, in summer, Waimea can be like a lake, with sailboats riding peacefully at anchor in the bay.

Behind the bay, occupying a narrow valley, Waimea Falls Park is laid out like a botanical garden, with a large waterfall and pool at its end. Admission is charged. Just before entering the gate to the park, *Hale o Lono Heiau* stands guard. Consecrated to *Lono*, the god of agriculture and harvests, the *heiau* has been restored, and can be seen at the far end of the visitor parking lot.

Three and a half miles from Waimea Bay, the road forks. To the left a new road bypasses the town of Haleiwa and continues on to Honolulu. The scenic drive takes the right fork at a sign proclaiming "Historic Haleiwa Town." Haleiwa (population 2,500) is the more developed of the two towns on the north shore and is a popular tourist stop as well as the local shopping center for area residents. It has a variety of surfing and tourist shops, several restaurants, two supermarkets, gas stations, and banks, but no accommodations. An excellent shoreline campground is located at Kaiaka Bay County Park on Haleiwa Road.

Once through Haleiwa, HI 83 ends at a traffic circle. Driving straight through the circle picks up HI 930, which, after 1 mile, turns right at a T junction and enters Waialua (population 4,000). The town has only recently acquired its "former plantation town" status. Waialua Sugar Company, the last plantation on Oahu, ceased production in 1996, and the large sugar mill, occupying a prominent position in the town, is closed. The work force of mostly Filipino ancestry is still in an uncertain transition. In the hills above town, along Highway 803, experimental plots of coffee, macadamia nuts, and vegetables are being grown, and there is talk of a large-scale forest industry.

Leaving Waialua, HI 930 proceeds in a straight line. Ranches, small farms, and former cane acreage occupy the land between the mountains and

Pounding winter shorebreak at Waimea Bay keeps swimmers out of the water.

the sea. The mountains on the left are the Waianae Range, which ends at Kaena Point. Just past the Mokuleia Polo Field, 4 miles from Waialua, a private campground is located at Camp Mokuleia, an attractive waterfront location. Dillingham Airfield begins here, its runway paralleling the highway. Glider rides and parachute jumps may be arranged. The Kealia Trail (7 miles round-trip) climbs from the west end of the airfield to the summit of the Waianae, for a sweeping view of the leeward coast. Opposite the airfield, Mokuleia County Beach Park also offers camping. In spite of its proximity to the highway, the 3-mile stretch of beach from here to the end of the pavement is one of the most isolated on Oahu, rarely visited except by shoreline fishermen and beachcombers.

One mile past the airfield, another private campground is located within the YMCA's Camp Erdman, on the ocean. Cabins can be rented here as well. The pavement ends about 1 mile past Camp Erdman, and a barrier across the road prevents further vehicle traffic. A rough jeep track continues along the coast to Kaena Point Natural Area Reserve, and hikers and bicycles are welcome. It is a 6-mile round-trip from the end of the pavement to the lighthouse at the point. A few bridge abutments from the old railroad can be seen along the jeep track. This wild, windswept place is ideal for beachcombing and shoreline exploration. Some rare beach plants grow only here, and at a few other locations in the Hawaiian Islands. The reserve is a nesting ground for sea birds, including the Laysan Albatross. Green sea turtles also nest here. The Hawaiian Monk Seal occasionally comes ashore here to bask on the beach.

Waialua Sugar Mill. The plantation closed in 1996, the last sugar operation on Oahu. In the background is Mt. Kaala, 4,020 feet, the highest point on Oahu.

MAUI

Maui is the second largest of the Hawaiian Islands and the second most visited after Oahu. The island is named for the demigod *Maui*, whose prodigious feats include pulling the Hawaiian Islands up from the bottom of the ocean, capturing the sun, raising the sky, and bringing fire to mankind.

The island of Maui was once much larger, encompassing the now individual islands of Molokai, Lanai, and Kahoolawe, which geologists call Maui Nui (Big Maui). Politically, Maui Nui still exists, as these four islands today form the County of Maui. Maui Island, formed by two volcanoes, Haleakala and Puu Kukui, is between 800,000 and 1.3 million years old. Puu Kukui, which formed West Maui, is one of the world's wettest locations, with an average rainfall of over 400 inches.

In the mid-nineteenth century, at the height of the whaling industry, Maui became the whaling capital of the Pacific. In 1846 more than four hundred whaling ships visited Maui, and as many as one hundred might be anchored off the Lahaina roadstead at one time. In the early nineteenth century Lahaina was the capital of the kingdom of Hawaii. But with the discovery of petroleum in Pennsylvania in the 1860s, the whaling industry collapsed, Maui languished, and the focus of activity moved to Honolulu. With the coming of sugar to the islands, Maui boomed again, as large plantations spread throughout its fertile lands. And, following the Second World War, tourism brought the greatest boom of all.

Maui's topography provides some of the best scenic driving in Hawaii. The massive slopes of Haleakala on East Maui offer thousands of acres of rain forest, countless waterfalls, and sweeping pasture lands. Its summit reveals a world of cinder cones and lava—high above the timberline, yet easily accessible by car. West Maui's deeply incised valleys form a dramatic backdrop for some of the most beautiful beaches anywhere in the world. Just a short distance from these popular watering spots, the coast turns wild, precipitous, and deserted, while remaining accessible to drivers. Much of Maui's great beauty can be seen from its dramatic highways and roads.

Area: 729 square miles
Population: 101,000
Airports: **Main**: Kahului. **Secondary**: Kaanapali, Hana.
Rental car offices: Kahului Airport, Kaanapali (limited), Hana (limited).

4

Haleakala National Park: From the Sea to the Summit

General description: This 40-mile drive begins in Kahului at sea level and rises to the rim of Haleakala Crater at 10,023 feet. Highlights include: spectacular views of Maui, the seacoast, outlying islands, and the interior of the crater.

Special attractions: Haleakala Crater, Hosmer Grove Nature Trail, *nene* (Hawaiian state bird), silverswords, Makawao town, Paia town, hiking, backpacking, camping.

Location: Central part of East Maui.

Drive route numbers: Hawaii Highways 37, 377 (Haleakala Highway), 378 (Haleakala Crater Road), 400, 390 (Baldwin Avenue), 36 (Hana Highway).

Camping: Four campgrounds—Hosmer Grove (no permit required), Rainbow County Park, H. A. Baldwin, and Kanaha Beach County Parks (permits required)—are located along the route. Two others, Holua and Paliku, are within Haleakala Crater and are accessible only on foot (permits required).

Services: Kahului: all services (major hotels, restaurants, shopping centers, auto service and repair, etc.). Pukalani: restaurants, gas, and limited shopping. Makawao: restaurant, gas, limited shopping. Some upcountry accommodations and restaurants. No services elsewhere on the route.

Nearby attractions: Kula ranch country, Polipoli Springs State Recreation Area.

 The drive

Beginning in Kahului (population 17,000), the drive traverses coastal sugar cane fields, upland pastures, high forests, and finally breaks out above the timberline to the barren cinder landscape of Haleakala summit. Dramatic scenery unfolds at virtually every turn of the road.

According to an ancient Hawaiian legend, Maui, the demigod, was responsible for dredging the Hawaiian Islands up from the bottom of the sea. Standing atop Haleakala, Maui also captured the sun, holding it prisoner until it agreed to slow down its daily trip across the sky. Haleakala National Park's 28,655 acres stretch from the highest point on Maui to the ocean over 20 miles away and include the entire crater of the massive, dormant volcano, which last erupted in 1790.

Haleakala National Park:
From the Sea to the Summit

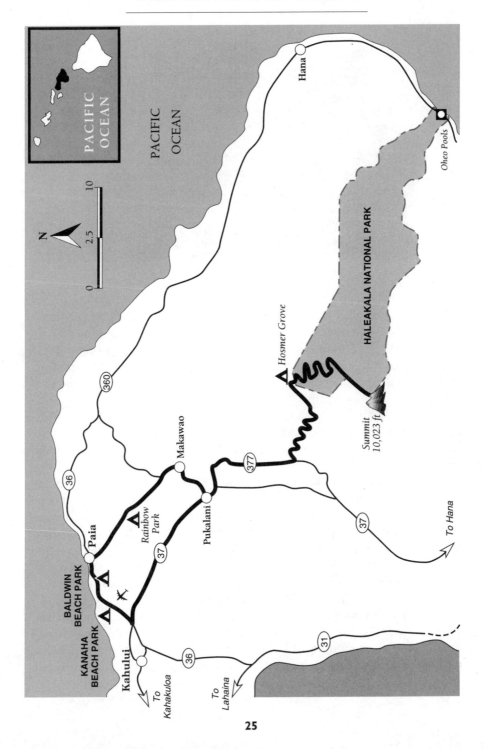

Sliding Sands Trail descends into the crater.

Weather on the mountain can be unpredictable. Bright sun, fog, rain, and high winds can be expected any time of the year—and sometimes all on the same day. The summit is usually cool and windy, even on sunny days. Temperatures range from 26 to 77 degrees Fahrenheit, with below freezing readings in the predawn hours when many tourists wait to watch the sun rise.

Leaving Kahului to the east on HI 37, the drive passes through wide fields of sugar cane. Once grown on all the main islands, sugar survives now only on Maui and Kauai, and even here the plantations face an uncertain future. Sugar, Hawaii's dominant industry for over 100 years, changed the face of the islands forever. Workers brought in from China, Japan, and the Philippines to perform field labor that Hawaiians refused to do, soon outnumbered the original inhabitants and superimposed their own cultures on the existing Polynesian society, virtually submerging it. It was sugar that was responsible for the annexation of Hawaii by the United States in 1898, when a cabal of Caucasian businessmen saw it as the only way to get favorable U. S. quotas for Hawaiian sugar. Having held the stage for well over a century, sugar now stands on the verge of passing into history.

Seven miles from the start of the trip, HI 37 passes through the town of Pukalani (population 6,000), where sugar gives way to lush, upland pastures. This is the beginning of Kula, Maui's cool, rich, ranch country. Half a mile later the drive turns left on HI 377, and after another 6 miles turns left

Northeast wall of the crater.

again on HI 378. Here the 12-mile long, steep switchback up the mountain begins. The road will climb nearly 8,000 feet in 20 miles, the world's steepest rise for a paved road over such a short distance. But the drive is neither dangerous nor difficult; the road is wide, and the curves are banked.

As the drive proceeds upward, sloping fields of grass cover the mountainside, interspersed with clumps of tall trees. At the park entrance, about halfway to the summit, a four dollars per car fee is charged, which is good for a week. Golden Age/Access Passes are honored. A turnoff to the left leads to Hosmer Grove (6,800 feet), a pretty, sheltered glen in a tall forest. A picnic area, campground, and a nature loop trail are located here. The campground requires no reservations or fee.

The grove is named for forester Ralph Hosmer, who planted it in 1910, hoping to start a local timber industry. Hosmer introduced trees from around the world, including pine, fir, spruce, and cypress from North America, eucalyptus from Australia, and Sugi from Japan. Although most of the imported trees have adapted to their new home, many of them do not grow as well as in their native lands; thus timber farming never became established on Maui.

Returning to HI 378 from Hosmer Grove, Park Headquarters lies 0.6 mile ahead. It has restrooms, drinking water, park information, maps, and guidebooks. Three miles farther on another turnoff from HI 378 leads to the parking lot for the Halemauu Trailhead at 8,000 feet. A 2-mile round-trip hike part way down the trail reaches a sweeping lookout over the crater and the Koolau Gap, where lava once poured out of the crater and flowed to the sea.

The Hawaiian state bird, the *nene*, makes its home on the mountain, and can often be seen in the trailhead parking lot. An upland goose, the *nene* is found only in Hawaii. Now a protected species, the bird is making a slow comeback from near extinction, caused by human and animal predators. Propagation stations, where young geese are raised and then released into the wild, have had only partial success.

Returning once again to HI 378, the drive passes two more overlooks of the crater that are worth a stop, Leliwi and Kalahaku. At 9,000 feet, lava fields take over from the dwindling grass, and at 9,600 feet, brown cinder makes its appearance. Brown cinder is the dominant landscape feature of the summit and the crater. A large parking lot announces the visitor center, poised on the crater's edge at 9,745 feet. Farther up the road, near the actual summit, Puu Ulaula Overlook offers a bigger building with large glass windows. Here visitors can admire a strikingly beautiful feature of the park, the silversword, a plant which grows nowhere else in the world. Blooming only once in its up to twenty-year life span, the silver-gray plant thrusts up a spike covered with a hundred or more flowers and then dies. The

Blooming silversword will soon wither and die, like the stalk on the right.

silversword was once threatened with extinction by voracious herds of goats, but fencing of the crater and elimination of the goats has allowed the plant to make a successful comeback. The observatory structures at the end of the road are scientific facilities and are not open to the public.

From Puu Ulaula, the view is awe-inspiring. Almost the entire chain of islands is on display: Hawaii, Kahoolawe, Lanai, Molokai, and sometimes even Oahu, are all visible on a clear day. And below the overlook, an immense crater, 19 square miles and 2,700 feet deep, sweeps across the landscape. Cinder cones that seem relatively small from here, actually tower up to 600 feet from the crater floor. Haleakala is not a true volcanic crater, but an erosional depression, formed by centuries of rain and wind. Post-erosional eruptions have restored its volcanic appearance.

Sliding Sands Trail, which starts to the right of the parking lot, descends to the floor of the crater and connects to its network of trails. A short hike down the trail, or the 5-mile round-trip to Kaluu o ka O'o, the summit of one of the crater's cinder cones at 8,200 feet, is an excellent way to experience the feel of this strange world.

The drive descends the mountain by the same route, back to the town of Pukalani. Even though you are retracing the drive, new vistas and perspectives appear all the way down the mountain. At Pukalani, the route turns right on HI 400 for 2.3 miles to Makawao (population 5,400), the *paniolo* capital of Maui's ranch country. *Paniolo* are Hawaii's cowboys. The name originates from "Espaniolo," the term given to the islands' first ranch hands, who came from Spain and Mexico. The small town's weather-beaten, false-front buildings are reminiscent of the Old West.

From Makawao, the drive turns left on Baldwin Avenue. About 3 miles from town is Rainbow Park, a small picnic and camping area located in a hollow on the left side of the road. It then passes a functioning sugar mill in Paia and reaches the coast at Lower Paia, another false-front town. At the intersection of HI 36, the drive turns west (left), returning to Kahului. En route, it passes H. A. Baldwin and Kanaha beach parks, both of which offer campgrounds.

5
The Hana Highway,
Oheo Pools, and the South Shore

General description: This 110-mile coastal drive is one of the most diverse in the Hawaiian Islands. It circles the base of Haleakala, Maui's huge, dormant volcano, passing lush rain forests, waterfalls, streams, and pools. It then visits the town of Hana and the Kipahulu section of Haleakala National Park (Oheo Pools), traverses the island's dry and virtually deserted south shore, and finally ends in Maui's upland ranch country. Although the trip can be made in one day, to get the most out of the experience, an overnight stop should be made in Hana.

Special attractions: Paia town, Hookipa Beach Park, Waikamoi Ridge Nature Trail, Keanae Arboretum, Keanae Valley Lookout, Puaakaa State Wayside, Waianapanapa State Park and Caves, Hana, Oheo Pools, Charles A. Lindbergh's Grave, Kaupo Gap, Tedeschi Winery, hiking, backpacking, camping, swimming, snorkeling, scuba, surfing, sailboarding, boating, kayaking, fishing, beachcombing.

Location: Eastern portion of the island of Maui.

Drive route numbers: Hawaii Highways 36, 360 (Hana Highway), 31 (Piilani Highway), 37 (Kula Highway).

Camping: Four campgrounds are located along the route: Kanaha Beach County Park, H. A. Baldwin Beach County Park, Waianapanapa State Park, and the Kipahulu Section of Haleakala National Park (Oheo Pools). Permits are required for the first three, but not for Kipahulu.

Services: Kahului: all services (major hotels, restaurants, shopping centers, auto service and repair, etc.). Paia: restaurants, gas, and limited shopping. Hana: accommodations, gas, and limited shopping. A beach snack bar and a small restaurant are open for lunch only. The restaurant at the Hana Maui Hotel serves three meals daily. Pukalani: restaurants, gas, and limited shopping. There are no services available along the route.

Nearby attractions: Twin Falls, Keanae, Nahiku, *Piilanihale Heiau*, Kahanu Gardens, "Blue Pool," Red Sand Beach.

 The drive

In its first 52 miles, on the Hana Highway, the drive rounds over 600 curves, crosses 56 bridges, and passes several waterfalls, all the while displaying spectacular coastal and mountain views. Driving east on HI 36 from Kahului, the route passes the airport and the entrance to Kanaha Beach County Park, which has a campground. The drive crosses waving fields of sugar cane, and then follows the coast. H. A. Baldwin County Beach Park offers another campground.

Six miles from Kahului, Paia, a former plantation town, has boutiqued itself with pastel-colored shops and false-front buildings, successfully attracting tourist eyes and tourist pocketbooks. Three miles farther, Hookipa Beach Park lures sailboarders from all over the world. If the winds are up, it is worth stopping to watch the world's best sailboarders in action. At the intersection of HI 365, HI 36 becomes HI 360, the official Hana Highway. Mile-posting signs start over at this point.

At the Hoolawa Bridge (2-mile marker), a mile-long foot trail leads to Twin Falls, a pretty spot with a small pool. The trail begins at a stile over a fence on the right side of the road, near a "No Trespassing" sign that everyone ignores. Farther down the road, between mileposts 9 and 10, is another possible diversion, the Waikamoi Ridge Trail Nature Walk, a mile-long loop trail through a rain forest. It begins on the right side of the highway. At mile marker 11, the drive reaches Puohokamoa Falls, which tumbles into a small pool easily seen from the road. Kaumahina State Wayside, a rest stop, has drinking water, restrooms, and picnic tables. A lookout on the eastern side of the wayside provides a fine view of the Keanae Peninsula. After Kaumahina, HI 360 hugs the mountain—steep walls of rock rising on one side, sheer sea cliffs dropping off on the other as it descends to Honomanu Bay—only to rise precariously again after crossing Honomanu Stream. Careful driving is required here; portions of the road are very narrow, especially on the curves, and many sections are one-way.

Another worthwhile detour, about 3 miles from Kaumahina, is a road off HI 360 which descends to the small village of Keanae on the peninsula of the same name. Here, residents, many of Hawaiian ancestry, fish, grow taro, and live a partly self-sufficient lifestyle. The peninsula provides colorful seascapes and a fine view of Haleakala.

The Keanae Arboretum, at milepost 16, displays hundreds of tropical plants, shrubs, and trees. An entire section is devoted to palms and another to plants introduced by the original Hawaiian settlers. Also on the grounds are several functioning taro paddies. An upper section of the arboretum, reached by a rough trail, is devoted to native and introduced rain forest plants. There are no facilities on the grounds. Admission is free.

Returning to HI 360, the Wailua Wayside Overlook lies just under 0.5 mile from the Keanae turnoff. A short trail leads to a view of the Koolau Gap, a huge rent in the wall of Haleakala Crater, where ancient lavas once poured from the volcano to the sea. This massive spillway is now completely covered by vegetation. The nearby staircase leads to a sweeping view of the coast and Keanae Peninsula. Three miles farther, at Puaakaa State Wayside, there are two small pools connected by a waterfall. Rest rooms, drinking water, and picnic tables are available.

The Hana Highway, Oheo Pools, and the South Shore

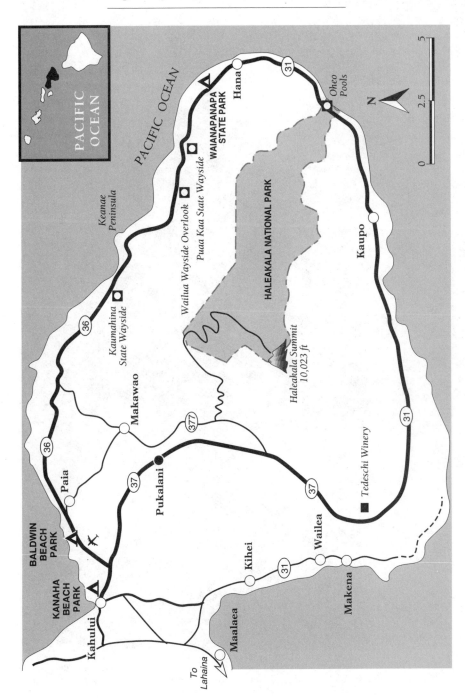

Oheo Pools, a very popular spot in the Kipahulu District of Haleakala National Park, is a series of ponds and small waterfalls formed by Oheo Stream as it makes its way to the sea.

The drive now begins to gradually straighten, the side of the highway becomes less precipitous, and pasture land starts to intrude on the rain forest. Waianapanapa State Park, just past the Hana Airport turnoff, is a good place to stop for the night, offering a campground and low-cost state cabins. The town of Hana is only 2 miles farther down the road. The oceanside park features black sand and a lovely cove for swimming. Two large caves within the park are collapsed lava tubes, partly filled with fresh water; it is possible to swim in the upper one. A sign at the upper cave tells the story of a Hawaiian princess who used the cave to hide from her jealous husband who suspected her of having an affair with another man. The husband saw her reflection on the water and killed her. Ever since, the legend goes, the pool turns red at certain times of the year.

Also leading through the park is an *alaloa*, an ancient footpath connecting towns and villages in the coastal area. *Alaloa* existed on all of the islands, and are sometimes called the "King's Highway," in honor of the rulers of Hawaii who had them built for communication and the convenience of the King's tax gatherers. Maui is the only island on which *alaloa* completely circled the coastline. Today it remains the island with the only complete coastal road. The southern section of the trail leads all the way to Hana, crossing spectacular coastal scenery, where waves crash against rocky cliffs, sending spray showering over hikers walking the path.

In spite of the fact that many visitors to Maui seem to consider a trip to Hana much like a journey to Mecca, Hana is a fairly ordinary small Hawaiian town. It has a beach park on Hana Bay, a small museum, two churches, two stores, a luxury hotel, some other accommodations, and not much else. But for those with the time to do so, an overnight stay here is recommended to provide the leisure to stop at points of interest along the drive and to enjoy the surrounding area. The Hasegawa General Store, which had a song composed for it and is well known to old-time Hana travelers, is no more. It burned down several years ago. The new store is more modern, but not as picturesque or as interesting as the old one, which stocked everything from matches to machetes.

Hana Beach Park, with its brown sand beach, is attractively located on Hana Bay. Kaahumanu, the favorite wife of Kamehameha, was born in a nearby cave. A short trail at the end of the road leads to the cave. At the time of her birth, a war was raging between Maui and Hawaii, and her family was hiding in the cave. After Kamehameha's death Kaahumanu became regent during the reigns of Kamehameha's two sons, and for thirteen years was the most powerful figure in the kingdom. Initially opposed to Christianity, she eventually converted, providing a major impetus to its spread throughout the islands.

A side trip from Hana allows a visit to *Piilanihale Heiau*, the largest temple in the Hawaiian Islands. It is located on the grounds of Kahanu Gardens, about 4 miles north of town, on Ulaino Road. The gardens are only open on certain days and times, and there is an admission charge. Call 808-248-8912 for information. Driving past the gardens to the end of Ulaino Road, and continuing on foot across the stream and then a few hundred yards along the coast, reveals Blue Pool, a fresh water pool fed by a wide waterfall trickling over a wide rock wall.

Another great place to visit while in Hana is *Kaihalulu*, better known as Red Sand Beach. Here, in a secluded cove, red cinders have washed from the hillside to form a unique beach. It is a dramatic setting. Waves pounding in from the open ocean are blocked by a natural breakwater, leaving a large inshore pool that is usually safe for swimming.

To find Kaihalulu, head toward Hana Bay. Just before reaching the bay, turn right at the last crossroad, pass the school and park near the end of the road before the hotel cottages. Cross the open grassy field on the left, walking diagonally toward the ocean. At the corner of the hotel fence, a trail leads steeply downhill and then turns left, following the shoreline to the beach. Due to its seclusion, nudists sometimes frequent this beach.

Departing from Hana, the drive proceeds south on HI 31 (Piilani Highway), passing through small, rural settlements and beautiful coastal scenery. The road soon becomes narrow and winding, but despite its condition it is heavily traveled. Many celebrities own homes and estates along this route, but they are not visible from the road. About 6 miles from Hana, the drive crosses a bridge where Wailua Falls drops into a gorge below. Traffic often jams up here as people stop to take photographs.

Ten miles from Hana, the route enters the Kipahulu Section of Haleakala National Park, with its famous Oheo Pools. Many of them are dramatically visible on both sides of the bridge where the drive enters the park. At the parking lot (on the left after crossing the bridge), a path leads to the lower pools. Swimming is safe in the pools except during periods of heavy rain or very high water; ocean swimming in this area is dangerous.

For many years, this area was known as Seven Sacred Pools, although the pools were never sacred and there are a good deal more than seven of them. It is a catchy phrase, apparently invented to attract tourists to the Hana area, and is rightfully fading from use. A campground is located here, and although rest rooms are available, there is no drinking water. No permit or fee is required.

Almost all of the upper part of Kipahulu Valley is a scientific reserve, closed to the public. However, across from the parking lot, a trail leads uphill to Makahiku Falls Overlook and Waimoku Falls, a 4-mile round-trip hike to a lovely bridal veil falls. On the way, the trail passes through a tall bamboo forest so thick that it blots out the sky.

From the Oheo Pools the drive continues to Palapala Hoomau Church, just over a mile from the pools. Charles A. Lindbergh, the man who made the first non-stop, solo, transatlantic flight, is buried here. A longtime resident of Kipahulu, the famed "Lone Eagle" personally selected this isolated spot as his last resting place. The route for the next 6 miles to Kaupo is narrow and winding, requiring slow, careful driving. Traffic is sparse, but meeting another vehicle on this section usually requires that someone back up. The coastal scenery is wild and dramatic.

Four miles from the Oheo Pools the pavement ends, and a rough gravel road takes over for the next 4.5 miles. At the small settlement of Kaupo, a store is the only structure on the highway. The store keeps erratic hours and will probably be closed. Upslope from the road looms the Kaupo Gap, a giant crack in the wall of Haleakala Crater that in ancient times spilled huge lava flows all the way to the sea. Leaving Kaupo, the road remains very narrow for another 2 miles.

When the pavement begins again, the road widens and remains so. After about 16 miles on the paved road, the drive reaches the southwest tip of Maui, at an elevation of 2,000 feet. Here, a sweeping view of the ocean and four islands unfolds—Molokai to the north, Lanai and Kahoolawe to the west, and the crescent-shaped islet of Molokini, below, just offshore. Directly below the highway, lies La Perouse Bay and the lava fields from the last eruption on Maui, which took place around 1790. The bay was named

Alau Island, a seabird sanctuary off the Maui coast, south of Hana.

The Kaupo Gap, a huge rent in the wall of Haleakala Crater, once poured millions of tons of lava from the 10,000-foot-high mountain to the sea.

for a French explorer, who was the first foreigner to come ashore on Maui. After his ships left the island, they visited Australia, then disappeared, and he was never heard from again.

The drive now turns north and enters the fertile farm and ranchlands of Kula. The cool climate here is ideal for nurturing certain flowers and vegetables, such as protea, lettuce, cabbage, and the famous Maui onions. At Ulupalakua Ranch, HI 31 becomes HI 37, which it will remain for the 23 miles back to Kahului. The tasting room of the Tedeschi Winery, located in a former jail, allows you to sample and buy its red and white wines, champagne, and pineapple wine. This is one of only two wineries in the islands; the other is located in the town of Volcano, on the island of Hawaii.

The route now becomes a delightful 15-mile drive through upcountry Maui, passing through small towns and lush pastures, while providing marvelous panoramic views of land and sea all the way to the West Maui mountains. The drive ends with the return to Kahului.

6

West Maui Circle and Iao Needle

General description: This 62-mile loop circles the West Maui Mountains and contrasts one of Maui's most developed coasts with one of its wildest and most isolated. As described here, the drive begins and ends in Kahului. However, you may begin at any point along the loop. You can take it in either direction.

Special attractions: Iao Needle, Olowalu petroglyphs, Lahaina, Kahakuloa town, hiking, camping, swimming, snorkeling, scuba, surfing, sailboarding, boating, kayaking, fishing, whale-watching.

Location: Western Maui.

Drive route numbers: Hawaii Highways 330, 30 (Honoapiilani Highway), and 340 (Kahekili Highway).

Camping: Three campgrounds lie along the route: Papalaua Beach County Park, Camp Pecusa, and Windmill Beach. Camp Pecusa is privately run; the other two require permits.

Services: Kahului/Wailuku, and Lahaina: all services (major hotels, restaurants, shopping centers, auto service and repair, etc.). Kaanapali: accommodations, restaurants, shopping. There are no services elsewhere on the route.

Nearby attractions: Kihei beaches.

 The drive

The route makes a complete circle of the West Maui Mountains, generally following the coast except for the portion across the isthmus between East and West Maui. West Maui's highest peak, Puu Kukui (5,788 feet), is one of the world's wettest spots, with rainfall averaging 400 inches per year. Coastal areas of West Maui, on the other hand, get much less. Lahaina, for example, receives only 14 inches.

The drive begins by proceeding west from Kahului (population 17,000) on HI 32, which after the intersection with HI 30 becomes Iao Valley Road. It continues 3 miles through the valley to Iao Needle, a sheer rock tower that rises 1,200 feet from the valley floor, and which many consider to be Maui's unofficial landmark. By watching for a small sign, a reasonably good likeness of John F. Kennedy in profile can be seen on the way into the valley. A staircase path ascends to an overlook affording a fine view of the Needle and the valley. Iao Valley was the scene of the battle in which Kamehameha defeated the forces of the chief of Maui, bringing the island under his rule. The water of the Iao Stream was said to have run red with the blood of fallen warriors.

Backtracking on Iao Valley Road, the drive turns right on HI 30 toward Lahaina. The route now crosses the isthmus between the two volcanoes which formed Maui, Haleakala on the east, and Puu Kukui to the west. Eight miles from Kahului, rounding McGregor Point, the islands of Molokini and Kahoolawe come into view. Papalaua County Beach Park, 4 miles farther on the left, has a campground which at the time of this writing was still under development. The ocean here is almost always calm, and the inshore area shallow. An offshore reef offers snorkeling and diving. Whales can often be seen out in the Au Au Channel between November and May.

Before reaching the small settlement of Olowalu (3.5 miles from Papalaua), the route passes Camp Pecusa, a private campground on the shoreline. In 1790 an infamous massacre of Hawaiian natives occurred at Olowalu. Simon Metcalf, captain of an American sailing ship, incensed over the theft of a stolen boat, lured the villagers out to his ship with the promise of trade and then opened fire, killing more than eighty people, and wounding hundreds. Seeking revenge for this atrocity, the local Hawaiian chief captured a ship commanded by Metcalf's son and slaughtered the entire crew, except for one man, whom he took prisoner. A short time later, Kamehameha captured the boatswain of Metcalf's ship. Both men, Isaac Davis and John Young, eventually became trusted advisors to the king.

An interesting petroglyph site lies about 0.5 mile inland from the highway, behind Olowalu Store. A dirt road through the cane fields toward the mountains leads to a platform along a cliff face on the right side of the road. Here, ancient rock carvings of human figures, dogs, and sails are clearly visible. Recently, a "No Trespassing" sign appeared at the entry to the dirt road from the highway. Visitors should inquire at the store to determine the current status.

At the outskirts of Lahaina, about 5 miles from Olowalu, the drive leaves HI 30, takes the first highway exit, and follows Front Street along the water to the old town. Lahaina, once the whaling capital, now the whale-watching capital of the islands, was also the capital of the Hawaiian kingdom from 1820 to 1845. The old part of town seems much like it must have been in whaling days, except that sailors carousing through the streets in search of saloons and sex have been replaced by tourists seeking mai tais and T-shirts.

The largest banyan tree in the islands covers almost an acre in a square opposite the Pioneer Inn, a marvelous, rickety, old-style hotel on the waterfront. The hotel has an interesting history. Once the administration building for a failed sugar plantation on Lanai, it was disassembled board by

West Maui Circle and Iao Needle

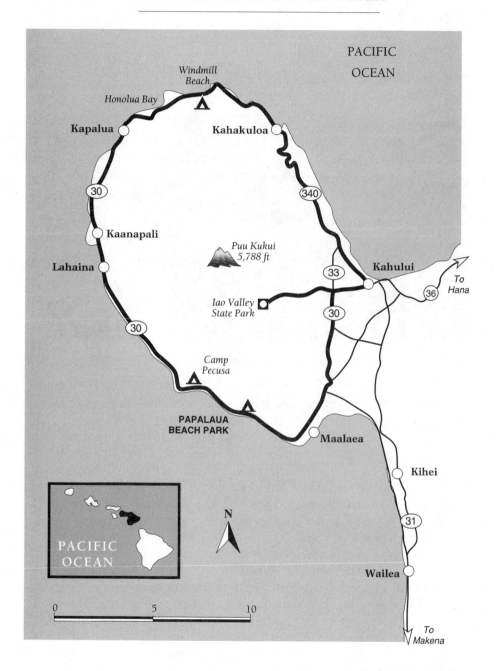

PACIFIC
OCEAN

Windmill
Beach

Honolua Bay

Kapalua

Kahakuloa

30

340

Kaanapali

Puu Kukui
5,788 ft

Lahaina

33

Kahului

To
Hana

36

Iao Valley
State Park

30

Camp
Pecusa

PAPALAUA
BEACH PARK

Maalaea

Kihei

PACIFIC
OCEAN

N

31

Wailea

0   5   10

To
Makena

Iao Valley's Needle soars skyward, creating Maui's most well-known landmark.

board, and rebuilt at its present location, where it has provided accommodations, food, and drink for almost one hundred years.

A self-guided walking tour of Lahaina's historic district takes in interesting buildings, a replica of an old sailing vessel, and a large Buddha in a cultural park in the northern part of town. In addition, lots of shops, art galleries, and restaurants are all within strolling distance of each other.

Leaving Lahaina, the drive rejoins HI 30 long enough to bypass the line of hotels along the beach at Kaanapali before turning off again, 3 miles from Lahaina, onto Old Route 30 which runs closer to the coast. It now passes clusters of condos and small hotels along the water, until it reaches Kapalua, a tastefully developed resort complex. The old road rejoins HI 30 just past D. T. Fleming Beach Park. Traffic decreases markedly for the remainder of the drive, but large cane-hauling trucks sometimes use the road, blaring their horns as they approach the curves. A mile from the junction, just after cresting a rise, cars parked in a cane field on the left may announce the start of a steep path to Honolua Bay, one of Maui's premier surfing spots. The inner portion of the bay also provides excellent snorkeling.

Shortly after Honolua, a dirt road descends to Windmill Beach, where camping is allowed with a permit from Maui Land & Pineapple Co. This is a primitive campsite, with no facilities of any kind. Two miles farther, HI 30 becomes HI 340, and the drive turns into a series of ups and downs and ins and outs as it winds around Maui's ruggedly beautiful northeastern coast. Not a single settlement or structure disturbs its isolation for 14 miles; until the tiny town of Kahakoloa, where less than 75 people live in a setting out of Hawaii's past. Most of these residents are of Hawaiian ancestry, and the town is one of the few places remaining in the islands where Hawaiian is still the main spoken language.

Nestled at the mouth of a deep valley, just behind a gray sand beach, Kahakuloa is framed by green mountains and high sea cliffs. In earlier times, the town was a favorite summer residence for high chiefs who indulged in the popular sport of *lele kawa*, or cliff diving. Kahekili's Leap, a jumping-off spot, is named for a chief who was particularly daring and fond of the sport. (There is another Kahekili's Leap on Lanai, see Scenic Drive 16). Both before and after the town, the road is *extremely* narrow and curving, requiring careful driving. Meeting another vehicle almost always means that one will have to back up.

Departing from Kahakuloa, a few houses begin to appear, well removed from each other. HI 340 continues to wind through rural scenery and coastal views, until it returns to Kahului.

As mentioned earlier, a pleasant side trip can be made which explores the marvelous beaches and rugged coastline of West Maui, from Kihei south to the end of the road at La Perouse Bay. The first part of this trip consists of the heavily developed areas of Kihei and Wailea, and from the road there is not much to see except condominiums and hotels. Although access to the shoreline seems cut off by all this development, public right of way exists for all the major beaches in the area. They are some of the best beaches found anywhere. The public access normally includes parking, and in some cases restrooms and showers. In Kihei, access is marked by square blue-and-white signs, while in Wailea, the beaches of Keawakapu, Mokapu, Ulua, Wailea, and Polo are marked with signs bearing their names. They are all fine beaches, and some of them have hotel-sponsored activities, such as snorkeling, scuba, surfing, and catamaran sailing.

The side trip begins at the intersection of HI 30 and HI 31, south of Kahului. It soon traverses a narrow strip of land with Maalaea Bay on the right and Kealia Pond, a seabird sanctuary, on the left. Just before entering Kihei, a choice of routes presents itself. HI 31 (Business) follows South Kihei Road, close to the coast, and affords access to the sea at beach parks and other locations. HI 31 proper becomes a divided highway, bypassing Kihei and paralleling South Kihei Road, but allowing access to it at only selected intersections. After 6 miles both routes come together again at the beginning of Wailea.

Figure of sailing captain at entrance to Pioneer Inn.

There is little of scenic interest on the bypass route; its advantage is a quick trip south for those who wish to avoid the congestion of Kihei. The Kihei South Road Route offers access to the coast and views of attractive sandy beaches, but requires a slower passage through typical outer-suburban sprawl—fast food restaurants, shopping malls, and traffic lights. Kihei's hotels and condos are more moderately priced than those of Kapalua to the north or Wailea to the south, and its atmosphere reflects this. Landscaping is not as lush, and buildings not as grandly designed, but it is Hawaii beachfront vacationing as many visitors want it to be, and it gives full value for the money.

When both routes rejoin at the beginning of Wailea, things become noticeably upscale. Gone are the shopping malls, gas stations and fast food emporiums. Landscaping rises to high art, and architecture to opulence (occasionally too much so). Huge sums have been spent here to lure the more affluent tourists, and it shows. Some of the plushest, most expensive hotels in the state line the coast for the next 5 miles, sharing world class golf courses and beaches (see above for beach access). The last hotel in this line of magnificence is the Maui Prince, perhaps the best designed of all in the way it blends gently into the land.

Once past the hotel, a dramatic change takes place. The coastline turns rocky, and the landscape becomes dry and open, with scrub brush and *kiawe*

The rooting branches of this 120-year-old banyan tree
in Lahaina cover almost an acre of ground.

trees predominating. No one is watering or manicuring here. Makena Landing, once the busiest port on Maui, now basks in obscurity about a mile south of the hotel. Puu Olai, a 360-foot-high cinder cone that has been visible along most of the route, pushes out into the ocean about another mile farther. Immediately south of Puu Olai is Makena State Park, which encompasses Oneloa Beach, a wide stretch of white sand more than 0.5 mile long. The north end of Oneloa is a low, rocky cliff, where a short trail leads to small Puu Olai Beach, nestled in a lovely setting. Although nudity is prohibited on Maui beaches, nudists often come to this secluded spot.

Leaving Oneloa, the road follows the rough shoreline of Ahihi Bay and enters the Ahihi-Kinau Natural Area Reserve, established on a portion of the last lava flow on Maui (circa 1790). A trail from a rough parking area leads to several boulder beaches and fine coastal views; snorkeling in these almost pristine waters is exceptional on days when the sea is calm. Entry from the rocky coast is difficult in most places and must be selected with care.

The road effectively ends at La Perouse Bay, about 3 miles from Oneloa. Even four-wheel-drive vehicles will have difficulty proceeding much farther. The bay was named for the French navigator who was the first westerner to set foot on Maui. A long portion of an *alaloa* (Hoapili Trail) begins here, but the coast is barren, hot, shadeless, and without drinking water.

Village of Kahakuloa.

HAWAII

Hawaii is by far the largest of the Hawaiian Islands—almost twice the size of all the others combined—earning its nickname, the "Big Island." Geologically speaking, it is the youngest of the islands, between 650,000 and a million years old—and it is still growing. Of the five volcanoes that formed the island, two, Mauna Loa and Kilauea, are still active. Kilauea, the most active volcano in the world, began its last eruption in 1983, and as of the date of this writing it was still going strong. It is also the world's only active drive-in volcano.

Hawaii was the first island to be settled by the Polynesians who discovered the chain. Kamehameha, the first chief to bring all the islands under one rule, was born, and died here. His grave lies hidden forever on the island. The famed explorer, Captain James Cook, the first westerner to find the islands, was killed here in an altercation over a stolen boat.

Hawaii's size and varied terrain provide a unique experience for auto tourists. Probably nowhere else in the world can one drive through such dramatically different landscapes in such a short space of time and distance. Verdant valleys, black sand beaches, alpine peaks, rain forests, rolling pastures, dry deserts, and lava fields—not to mention the volcano—all lie within a day's drive. Hawaii will amply reward the traveler who takes the time to enjoy its many wonders.

Area: 4,034 square miles
Population: 130,000
Airports: Main: Hilo, Kailua-Kona. **Secondary:** Waimea.
Rental car offices: Hilo Airport, Hilo, Kailua-Kona Airport, Waimea (limited).

7

Hilo, The Puna Coast, and the Volano's Fury

General description: This 76-mile loop begins and ends in Hilo, visits waterfalls, lava caves, a forest of lava-formed tree molds, the seismically active East Rift Zone of Kilauea Volcano, and explores the lava flows that have overrun the pretty seaside town of Kalapana.

Special attractions: Rainbow Falls, Boiling Pots, Kaumana Caves, Lava Tree State Park, Kalapana lava fields, hiking, camping, swimming, snorkeling, fishing.

Location: The easternmost portion of the island of Hawaii.

Drive route numbers: Hawaii Highways 200, 11, 130, 132, 137, and Pahoa-Pohoiki Road.

Camping: Three campgrounds are along the route: Isaac Hale Beach County Park, MacKenzie State Recreation Area, and Kalani Honua Conference and Retreat Center. The first two require permits, and the third is commercially operated.

Services: Hilo: all services (major hotels, restaurants, shopping centers, auto service and repair, etc.). Keaau and Pahoa: gas, restaurants, and limited shopping (small hotel in Pahoa). No services elsewhere on the route.

Nearby attractions: Pohoiki Warm Springs, Akaka Falls, Hawaii Volcanoes National Park.

 The Drive

Hilo (population 40,000) is the state's second largest city after Honolulu and the county seat for the Big Island. It is also the state's wettest town, with an average annual rainfall of 133 inches. All that rain makes Hilo lush, and it is the flower and ornamental plant capital of the islands.

In 1946 Hilo was struck by a *tsunami* (tidal wave) which reached 33 feet and caused 83 deaths in the town. Elsewhere on the Big Island, the wave reached as high as 55 feet, and island-wide deaths totaled 159. In 1960 another *tsunami* struck the town, reaching 38 feet, and killing 61 persons. Since then, warning systems have been developed, and evacuation of coastal areas should eliminate future fatalities. But the central part of Hilo, along the waterfront and the area most prone to *tsunami* flooding, has never been rebuilt. Today it is a park and a large expanse of green space.

Hilo, The Puna Coast, and the Volano's Fury

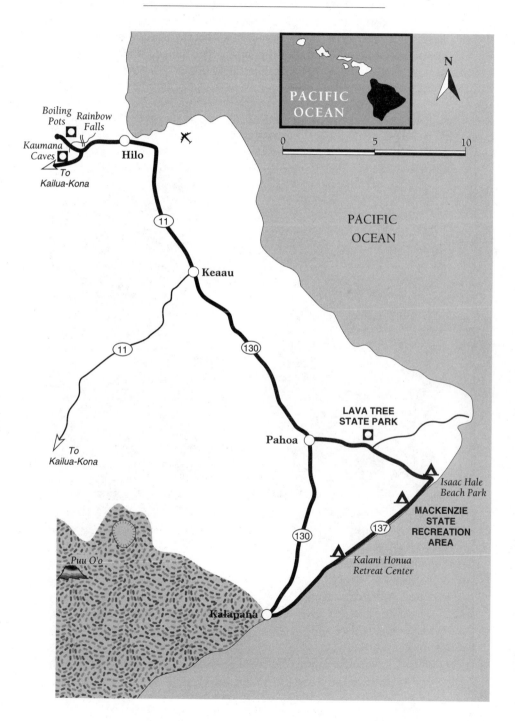

Boiling Pots
Rainbow Falls
Kaumana Caves
Hilo
To Kailua-Kona

PACIFIC OCEAN

11

Keaau

11

130

To Kailua-Kona

LAVA TREE STATE PARK

Pahoa

Isaac Hale Beach Park

MACKENZIE STATE RECREATION AREA

130

137

Puu O'o

Kalani Honua Retreat Center

Kalapana

PACIFIC OCEAN

N

0   5   10

The drive begins with a short trip to Rainbow Falls in the northwestern outskirts of town. Driving west on Kamehameha Avenue, the route turns left on HI 200, passes Hilo High School on the right, and then forks with HI 200 bearing left. The right fork, Waianuenue Avenue, leads to a sign for the falls, about 0.25 mile on the right. The falls can be viewed directly from the parking lot, or from a viewpoint reached by a short stairway. Just over 80

Rainbow Falls on the Wailua River, Hilo.

feet high, more than 300 million gallons of water pour over Rainbow Falls each day.

After the falls, the drive continues along Waianuenue Avenue for about 1.5 miles to Peepee Falls Street and turns right to Boiling Pots, which receives its name from swirling water cascading into a series of large pools. A steep trail descends to the river, and when the stream is not too high it is possible to walk out to some of the pools. Swimming is dangerous, as some of the rushing water leads to underwater tunnels that swimmers could be sucked into. The waterfall visible upstream from Boiling Pots is Peepee Falls.

The drive then returns along Waianuenue Avenue to the point where HI 200 turns off sharply to the right. Now following HI 200 for 3 miles, the drive comes to Kaumana Caves. Here, a stairway descends some 50 feet down a fern-filled pit, where a collapsed roof permits entry into two large lava tubes. A flashlight is needed to explore the tubes in depth, but the beginning reaches are accessible without one.

Reversing direction again from Kaumana, it is 4 miles back to the intersection of HI 200 and Kamehameha Avenue on the Hilo waterfront, where the drive turns right and proceeds 1.6 miles to the intersection of HI 11. Here, the drive turns right once more, for 8 miles to HI 130 and the town of Keaau. The drive then follows HI 130 for 10 more miles to the small, rickety town of Pahoa (entering the town itself, rather than using the bypass around it).

Pahoa, a collection of clapboard-front buildings, appears unlike other false-front towns, most of which are angling for tourist dollars. Pahoa seems old and tired, uninterested in tourists, and perhaps dreaming of the days when it was the marijuana capital of the Puna district. The weed is mostly gone now, but The Hemp Store survives, selling clothing and other products made from hemp cloth, and touting literature advocating the legalization of marijuana.

At the south end of Pahoa the road forks once more. The drive takes HI 132, the left fork (which seems like going straight ahead), for about 2.5 miles to Lava Tree State Park. Here, about two hundred years ago, a lava flow swept through a forest of large ohia trees, pooling against the large trunks. As the lava receded, it created grotesque shapes, formed when it surrounded the trees and burned them out. These "molds" still stand, and it is possible to peer down into some of them and see the imprint of the trees that burned long ago. The park has a covered picnic area, drinking water, and rest rooms.

Just past Lava Tree the road forks yet again, the drive leaves HI 132, bearing right on Pahoa-Pohoiki Road. For the next 4.5 miles the road winds through dense tropical growth until it reaches the seacoast at Isaac Hale Beach County Park. A campground is located here, with restrooms, but no drinking water. Pohoiki Warm Springs, a freshwater pond heated by volcanic action, is located a short distance from the campground. Starting at the caretaker's house, a walk toward the head of the bay along the shore leads to a short path into the vegetation and to the springs.

Turning right at Isaac Hale onto HI 137, the road soon narrows and begins to follow the sea. No tour buses and few other tourists will be seen. This is rural Hawaii as few people see it. Rain forest, coconut groves, and mango trees are interrupted by only a scattering of modest homes; and more development is unlikely. This is the the East Rift Zone of Kilauea Volcano, and homes and residents here are at the mercy of *Pele*, the goddess of fire, as will soon be evident.

Mackenzie State Recreation Area (2 miles past Isaac Hale) offers another campground and a picnic area in a forested grove, where black cliffs overlook the sea. There is no water here, and the restrooms are pit toilets. At milepost 19, Kehena Beach provides one of the few swimming spots on this coast. Nude bathers sometimes come here. Camping and other accommodations are available at Kalani Honua Conference and Retreat Center, 4 miles past MacKenzie.

Nine miles past MacKenzie, the road ends at the former junction of HI 137 and 130, now covered by lava flows. A paved connection has been reestablished between the two roads, allowing the itinerary to return to Pahoa via HI 130. The hardened lava fields and toppled palm trees that mark the end of HI 137 were once the town of Kalapana, a long-established village, which was destroyed in 1990. Kaimu Black Sand Beach, considered by many to be the prettiest in the state, once curved gracefully on the left, and now

New lava fields southwest of Kalapana on the Puna coast.

Entrance to the Kaumana Caves, a collapsed lava tube near Hilo.

lies buried forever under the same flows. Gone also are two subdivisions, two beach parks, and nearly three hundred homes and other structures. The loss of property exceeds $130 million, and probably has not ended. Kilauea, which began its current eruption in 1983, was still going strong at the time of this writing, although its activity was directed against uninhabited areas. But that could change at any time, if *Pele* once more turns her eye to the east.

It is possible to drive a few hundred yards more on HI 137 to a newly paved parking area, and a new store and snack bar. A walk up on the lava rise will reveal the vast extent of the volcano's destructive force. The drive now rejoins HI 130, but instead of immediately proceeding north toward Pahoa, turns temporarily left to a barrier across the road. Occasionally, a four-wheel-drive vehicle will be seen coming or going around the barrier, carrying supplies. The volcano spared a few homes in the area that are now completely surrounded by lava and cut off from all utilities. But some of their owners still use them, if only on a part-time basis. Prior to 1987 it was possible to continue southwest on HI 130 into the national park. But lava flows have now covered a 7-mile section of the road, severing the connection.

The drive now leaves the barrier, turns north on HI 130, and returns to Pahoa and Hilo.

8

Hawaii Volcanoes National Park: Craters, Cinder Cones, and Molten Lava

General description: This 50-mile drive circles the entire crater of Kilauea Volcano, then descends via the Chain of Craters Road to the coast to view active lava flows plunging into the sea.

Special attractions: Visitor center, Volcano Art Center, Kilauea Caldera, Jaggar Museum and Volcano Observatory, Halemaumau Fire Pit, Devastation Trail, Thurston Lava Tube, Kilauea-Iki Crater, Chain of Craters Road, Puu Loa petroglyphs, active lava flows, hiking, backpacking, camping.

Location: Hawaii Volcanoes National Park lies in the southeast portion of the island of Hawaii.

Drive route numbers: Crater Rim Drive, Chain of Craters Road.

Camping: Two vehicle-accessible campgrounds are located within the park, Namakani Paio and Kipuka Nene. They are free, and no permits are required. Cabins at Namakani Paio may be rented through the Volcano House Hotel. Backcountry cabins, shelters, and campgrounds are located throughout the park. They are free, but permits are required. Check with the visitor center.

Services: The Volcano House Hotel: accommodations, bar, restaurant, snack bar (located near the visitor center). Kilauea Military Camp (a recreation facility for military personnel and their families and guests, military ID required): accommodations, restaurant, gas, limited shopping. There are no other services in the park. The town of Volcano, one mile east of the park on Hawaii Highway 11, offers accommodations, restaurant, snack bar, gas, and limited shopping.

Nearby attractions: Rainbow Falls, Boiling Pots, Lava Tree State Park, Punaluu Black Sand Beach.

The Drive

Hawaii Volcanoes National Park encompasses more than 229,000 acres spread over 35 miles, from an altitude of 13,677 feet to sea level. The park may contain more vegetation zones than any other in the national park system. The center of most of the park's activity is Kilauea Crater. Although

The Rim Drive

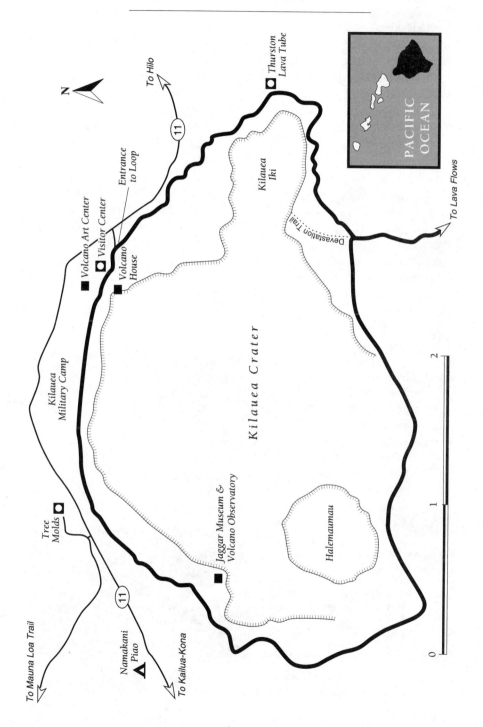

PACIFIC OCEAN

To Lava Flows

Thurston Lava Tube

Kilauea Iki

Devastation Trail

N

To Hilo

11

Entrance to Loop

Volcano Art Center
Visitor Center
Volcano House

Kilauea Crater

Kilauea Military Camp

Tree Molds

Jaggar Museum & Volcano Observatory

Halemaumau

To Mauna Loa Trail

Namakani Piao

11

To Kailua-Kona

0   1   2

the volcano has been constantly active since 1983, the eruption is currently taking place on its flank in the East Rift Zone, an area accessible only to knowledgeable and experienced hikers. However, lava flows from the eruption are entering the sea at the end of the Chain of Craters Road, and this area is reachable by car.

Kilauea Crater lies at an elevation of 4,000 feet, where days are usually warm, although they can be cool, especially when raining or windy. Nights are cool, ranging from 40 to 50 degrees Fahrenheit. The caldera area receives about 102 inches of rain per year. The park charges an admission of five dollars per person or ten dollars per car, which is good for seven days. Golden Age and Golden Access Passes are honored. The park is 28 miles from Hilo, via State Highway 11.

Since one of the main attractions of this trip is the active lava flowing along the seacoast, it is important to inquire about latest activity at the visitor center prior to departure. This itinerary can be easily modified to take advantage of the eruption, or to visit the flows at night. For venturing out on the lava flows, good walking shoes are advisable, and a flashlight is necessary after dark.

The drive begins at the visitor center, where Kilauea caldera dominates the immediate vicinity and the huge mass of Mauna Loa looms in the

Devastation trail as it appeared a few years after the eruption of Kilauea Iki in 1959. The forest has grown back considerably since then.

Hawaii Volcanoes National Park:
Craters, Cinder Cones, and Molten Lava

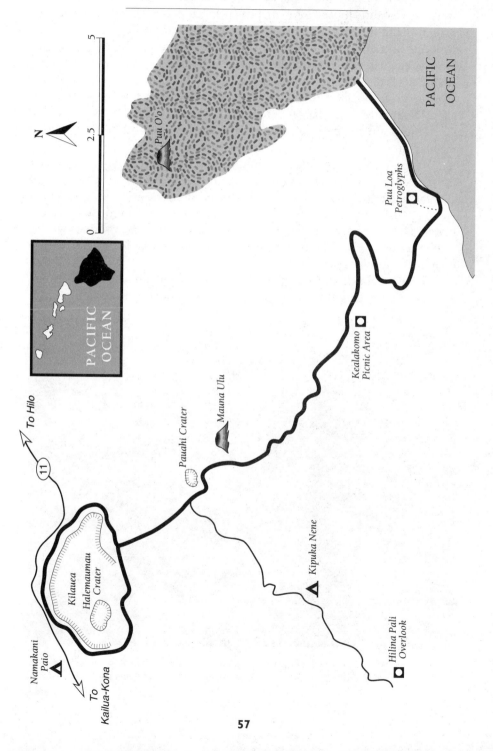

PACIFIC OCEAN

Puu O'o

Puu Loa Petroglyphs

PACIFIC OCEAN

Kealakomo Picnic Area

Mauna Ulu

Pauahi Crater

To Hilo

11

Kipuka Nene

Kilauea
Halemaumau Crater

Hilina Pali Overlook

Namakani Paio

To Kailua-Kona

N

0   2.5   5

distance. The center shows a film about the volcano every hour and books, maps, and brochures about the park are available. Directly across the highway, the Volcano House Hotel offers a spectacular view of Kilauea Crater.

Leaving the visitor center, the drive turns right on Crater Rim Drive, making short stops at the Sulphur Banks (0.3 mile on the right) and the Steam Vents (0.5 mile on the left). The route then passes Kilauea Military Camp, an R & R center for military personnel and their families. Kilauea Overlook, on the left, provides another fine view over the crater. The Volcano Observatory and Jaggar Museum, 2.5 miles from the visitor center, offers interesting displays and another crater overlook, this one with a good view down into Halemaumau, Kilauea's fire pit.

Continuing 3 more miles around Crater Rim Drive, a large parking lot on the left provides the opportunity to take a short walk to the rim of Halemaumau, the source of many of Kilauea's eruptions over the years. Flowers, fruit, or a bottle of Gordon's gin are sometimes seen on the edge of the crater. They are offerings to *Pele*, goddess of fire and the volcano, who is said to reside in Halemaumau. *Pele* reportedly has a taste for gin and a preference for Gordon's.

Leaving Halemaumau, the drive passes Keanakakoi Crater and enters a forest where the ground is still covered by cinders from an eruption of

Kilauea Iki Crater with Puu Puai, its cinder cone on the left. The lava fountain in 1959 rose an incredible 1,900 feet in the air forming the cone as the lava fell back to earth.

Kilauea Iki in 1959. The eruption blanketed the area to a depth of several feet and killed the original forest. The present forest sprang up after the eruption.

Two miles from Halemaumau, at the intersection of Chain of Craters Road, the drive turns right. Prior to 1986, this road became State Highway 130 when it left the park boundary, continuing to Kalapana and on to Hilo. On November 26th of that year the connection was severed by lava flows, which have continued to cover large segments of the park. Kilauea has since destroyed the park's Wahaula Visitor Center, Kamoamoa Campground, and Lae Apuki, the ruins of an old fishing village. At this writing, the lava barrier stands west of the Kalapana Trailhead, which has been overrun. Outside the park, the volcano has claimed the town of Kalapana, the Kaimu Black Sand Beach, two beach parks, and several subdivisions (see Scenic Drive 7).

Chain of Craters Road follows a line of pit craters formed in prehistoric time. The most interesting of these is Pauahi Crater, 3 miles from the intersection, where a wooden platform affords a view into the crater and of Mauna Ulu, the large lava mountain to the front. After Pauahi Crater, the drive pulls into the parking lot at Mauna Ulu (Growing Mountain). This imposing lava shield was formed by a large eruption lasting from 1969 to 1974, and is responsible for the huge solidified cascades of black lava that appear later along the route. A short walk toward Mauna Ulu reveals a remnant of the old Chain of Craters Road, which was covered by the 1969-1974 eruption. The present road is a rerouting of the old one.

A walk out on the lava fields to the left along the Napau Crater Trail passes among tree molds, formed when lava pounded against trees of the former forest and then receded. Looking down into some of them, it is still possible to see the impression of the tree trunk. Should an eruption be occurring at Puu O'o, the source of the current activity in the park, it can be viewed from the top of Puu Huluhulu, the swaybacked hill visible about a mile away, left of Mauna Ulu. The Napau Crater Trail, which begins near the parking lot, crosses the lava fields to the path leading to the top of Puu Huluhulu.

Back on Chain of Craters Road, the Kealakomo Picnic Pavilion, about 7 miles further down the road, commands an expansive view of the Puna coastline and its lava fields. (If this is a lunch stop, a resident mongoose may appear in the rocks below the right side of the pavilion sniffing for a handout.)

The drive now drops more steeply and makes a long hairpin turn. A pullout at the bottom of the descent allows an impressive look back at the black Niagara made by Mauna Ulu's lavas pouring over the Holei Pali. A 1.5-mile round-trip trail from the next pullout leads to the Puu Loa petroglyphs, a large field containing rock carvings of human figures, sails, circles, dots, and other objects. A boardwalk circles the fragile carvings to

Entrance to the Thurston Lava Tube on Crater Rim Drive.

prevent damage from foot traffic. The significance of these petroglyphs is unknown. They have been found on all islands, but the Big Island has far more than any other.

A mile past the Puu Loa pullout, the road reaches the sea and follows the coastline until it ends at a barrier staffed by park rangers. From here it is usually possible to walk to where the road has been cut by the latest lava flow. This is an area of constant change. The show depends on what *Pele* is up to that day, and what the rangers feel is safe. Sometimes it is possible to walk right up to lava flows pouring into the sea, sometimes not. At times the hillsides glow bright orange and vegetation bursts into flame just yards off the road. At other times there is nothing to see but tons of cooling black lava. When activity permits, temporary trails are marked out along the new flows, even as heat still radiates from their hot cores.

From the end of the road the drive returns along Chain of Craters Road back to Crater Rim Drive and proceeds directly across the drive to the Devastation Trail parking lot. A fifteen-minute walk along a boardwalk traverses an area where cinders from the 1959 eruption of Kilauea-Iki destroyed an entire forest. Most of the forest has regenerated now, and the walk is much less dramatic than it was twenty-five years ago, when it was a striking tour through hundreds of fallen trees, strewn like giant match sticks across a barren, cinder landscape. The walk ends at a viewpoint overlooking Kilauea Iki. The brown hill on the left is Puu Puai, the cinder cone formed by the 1959 eruption, where the fountaining lava spewed an incredible 1,900 feet into the sky.

Leaving the Devastation Trail parking lot the drive turns left, continuing along Crater Rim Drive 1.5 miles to Thurston Lava Tube. A short trail makes its way into a depression filled with lush vegetation and enters the illuminated lava tube from a collapsed roof. Lava tubes are formed by lava flows that cool and harden on the surface but continue flowing underground. When the flow finally ceases, the tube empties, leaving an underground passage. Many ancient Hawaiians used lava tubes as burial chambers.

Leaving the lava tube, the drive makes one more stop at Kilauea Iki Overlook, where it is just possible to pick out the trail crossing the center of the crater. Hikers may be visible on this trail, making a loop trip from Volcano House.

The drive now returns to the visitor center.

9

The Hamakua Coast, Parker Ranch Country, and the Mauna Kea-Mauna Loa Saddle Road

General description: This 140-mile loop begins and ends in Hilo. It follows Hawaii's lush Hamakua Coast to Waipio Valley Overlook, traverses portions of the vast Parker Ranch, visits the town of Waimea, and finally crosses the high, wide saddle between the two giant volcanoes—Mauna Kea and Mauna Loa. Two side trips, to the summit of Mauna Kea and to a weather observatory high on Mauna Loa, are possible during this tour.

Special attractions: Hamakua coastline, Saddle Road, Akaka Falls, Waipio Valley Lookout, Parker Ranch, Mauna Kea, Mauna Loa, hiking, backpacking, camping.

Location: The northeastern part of the island of Hawaii.

Drive route numbers: Hawaii Highways 19, 220, 190, and 200.

Camping: Three campgrounds are located along the route, Kolekole Beach and Laupahoehoe Beach county parks, and Kalopa State Recreation Area (permits are required). In addition, low-cost cabins can be rented at Kalopa and Mauna Kea state recreation areas.

Services: Hilo: all services (major hotels, restaurants, shopping malls, auto service and repair, etc). Waimea: two motels, restaurants, gas, and most shopping. Honokaa: one small hotel, food, gas, shopping. No other services are available along the route.

Nearby attractions: Rainbow Falls, Boiling Pots, Kaumana Caves, Onizuka Center for International Astronomy, Mauna Kea Summit, Mauna Loa Weather Observatory.

The Drive

This long but rewarding tour features dramatic changes in scenery. Beginning in the town of Hilo, the drive follows the Hamakua coast to the end of the road at Waipio Valley Overlook, then retraces part of the route, arriving in Waimea, heart of the famous Parker Ranch. From there, the drive heads south and returns to Hilo on the Saddle Road (HI 200) between Mauna Kea and Mauna Loa, crossing some of the most rugged lava fields on the island.

The Hamakua Coast, Parker Ranch Country, and the Mauna Kea-Mauna Loa Saddle Road

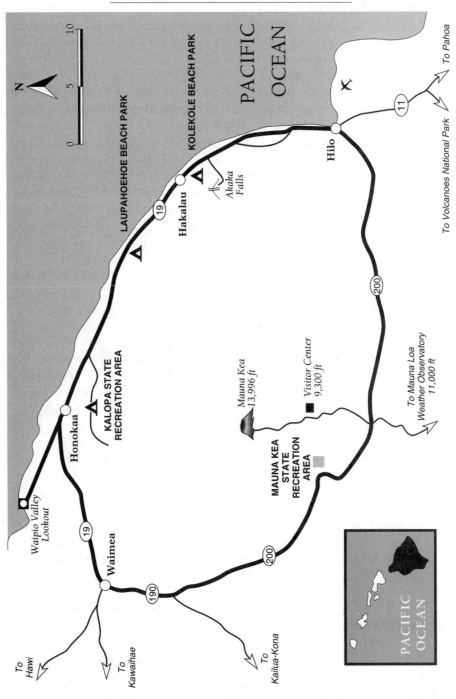

For a more leisurely trip, the drive can be extended to two days, providing ample time to explore and sightsee along the way, particularly if one or both of the side trips are planned (see below). In this case, Waimea is the logical stopover point.

Two optional side trips are available from the Saddle Road. The first travels up the side of Mauna Kea, either to a visitor center at 9,300 feet; or for those driving four-wheel-drive vehicles, to the summit at 13,796 feet, the highest point in the state. The second option is to drive to a weather observatory high on the slope of Mauna Loa (11,000 feet). Both options afford sweeping panoramic views over the surrounding countryside and the sea and are discussed in more detail below.

Some rental car companies have restrictions against driving on the Saddle Road. These restrictions make little sense, as the highway is better than some other roads in the state that have no such restrictions. (The Hana Highway on Maui, for example, has far more curves, is narrower in most places, precipitous in some, and has heavier traffic, yet no rental company restricts its use.) Parts of the Saddle Road are subject to early morning and evening fog, and during maneuver activity, large military vehicles use the western portion of the road. However, for those who manage to get around the driving restriction, the Saddle Road should present no unusual problems for a normally careful driver.

The Hamakua coast occupies almost 55 miles of Hawaii's windward shoreline. Dozens of gulches, streams, and waterfalls make their way down the slopes of Mauna Kea toward the sea, watering the miles of sugar cane fields that previously covered the landscape. This coast was once the domain of Hamakua Sugar Company, one of the largest plantations in the state. Struggling for years with profitability, Hamakua Sugar finally ceased operations in 1995. When the Ka'u Sugar Plantation to the south followed suit, sugar production on the Big Island, after 160 years of dominating the agricultural scene, passed into history. But small plantation towns still line the route, their inhabitants unsure of their future. Tentative plans for the former sugar lands include small vegetable farms, coffee, macadamia nuts, and a large forestry industry. As of the date of this writing, nothing had been finalized.

Leaving Hilo to the north on HI 19, the drive follows the shoreline of Hilo Bay a short distance before it leaves the water and begins to climb. For most of the trip, the highway travels high above the shoreline, which is only occasionally visible. The sea itself, however, is almost always in view. Shortly after the small town of Papaikou (4 miles from Hilo), the route forks right off the highway at a sign marked "Scenic Drive." The Hawaii Tropical Botanical Garden, near the beginning of the drive, offers tours for an admission fee. The road winds through dense stands of tropical trees and plants, crosses ponds and waterfalls over narrow bridges, and overlooks dramatic inlets. A particularly striking view is Onomea Bay, where a rocky promontory has split, and appears on the verge of plunging into the sea. The route rejoins HI 19 in about 4 miles.

Another 2 miles and the drive turns left onto HI 220, to visit Akaka Falls. After passing through the quaint plantation town of Honomu, the road rises steeply through former cane fields, now lying fallow and sprouting scattered wild clumps of new sugar cane that will never be harvested. At the falls parking lot, a paved walking trail descends through a botanical garden setting—lush plants, giant bamboo, and a huge banyan tree—to two striking waterfalls, Kahuna Falls, 400 feet high, and Akaka, with a 442-foot plunge.

Retracing HI 220 back to HI 19 and turning left, Kolekole Beach County Park quickly becomes visible on the right and below the highway. There is a campground here, and a small, attractive waterfall and pool. Two short side trips off HI 19, one at Hakalau, and the other at Laupahoehoe Beach County Park, offer close-up views of the coastline at sea level. There is a campground at Laupahoehoe, and a memorial to twenty-four students and teachers from a small schoolhouse who were swept out to sea by the *tsunami* of 1946.

Back on HI 19, and for the next 16 miles, small plantation towns continue to appear along the route, most of them little more than a structure or two on the highway, fading relics of an earlier time. Just before Honokaa, a road to the left climbs to Kalopa State Recreation Area, situated within an attractive upland rain forest. A campground and low-cost state cabins are located here.

At Honokaa, the drive temporarily leaves HI 19, bears right, and goes through the town 8 miles to the end of the road at Waipio Valley Lookout. Waipio, with its mile-long black sand beach, is the largest valley on the Big Island. The view from the lookout is one of the most scenic in the islands, attested to by the fact that when the survivors of the Kevin Costner megafilm, *Waterworld,* finally found land, it was at Waipio Valley that they came ashore. Once a thriving Hawaiian community, only a few people live here today. By the turn of the century, most of the population had departed for the cities. Those who remained were driven out by the two devastating *tsunami* of 1946 and 1960. It was at Waipio that the 1946 wave reached its crest—more than 55 feet.

Waipio places significantly in Hawaiian legend and history. It was a location favored by the gods, and Maui, the demigod, is believed to have died in the valley. (Maui is credited with creating the Hawaiian Islands by dragging them up from the sea.) Many powerful Hawaiian chiefs were born in Waipio, and here Kamehameha, first king of all the islands, was introduced to his war god, putting him on his path of conquest. More recently, in

Akaka Falls plunges 442 feet into a tropical pool.

1994, caskets containing the remains of two of ancient Hawaii's most renowned chiefs were stolen from the Bishop Museum where they had been in custody since 1918. There are indications that these sacred relics were taken from the museum to be returned to a secret burial place in the valley, where it is believed they were originally interred.

The road down to the valley floor can only be driven with a four-wheel-drive vehicle. The twenty-five percent grade is far too steep for the brakes and transmission of a standard car. It requires twenty to thirty strenuous minutes to walk down the road to the valley floor, and thirty to fourty-five even more strenuous minutes to walk back up. Waipio Valley Shuttle and Tours (808-775-7121) offers four-wheel-drive tours of the valley.

From Waipio Lookout, the drive returns to Honokaa via the same route and rejoins HI 19, turning right toward Waimea, about 12 miles away. A short climb through the tall, coastal forest, and the route breaks out into open, rolling country, where cattle graze contentedly in lush, green pastures. As the road approaches Waimea, small, rural ranches appear, finally giving way to homes, and then the town itself. Waimea, long the headquarters of the Parker Ranch, has more recently also become the support center for the astronomical observatories located on the summit of Mauna Kea.

The Parker Ranch was the largest privately owned cattle ranch in the United States until 1992, when its last owner, Richard Smart, died and left most of his assets to a charitable trust. The ranch got its start in the late 1700s, when British sea captain George Vancouver presented King Kamehameha with several head of cattle, hoping to found a ship-provisioning industry in the islands. The king placed a *kapu* (taboo) on the small herd, prohibiting anyone from harming the animals on pain of death. Over the years the cattle flourished to the point where they were trampling and destroying private crops, but nothing could be done because of the king's *kapu*.

It was then that John Parker, a former English seaman, proposed to the king that he be allowed to round up the cattle, restrict them to a small ranch, and begin increasing the herd through breeding. The king agreed, and over the years, by means of marriage, purchase, and lease, the ranch came into the hands of the Parker family. Today, it runs a herd of 50,000 Hereford cattle, as well as sheep, horses, and a dairy herd. It owns or leases more than 235,000 acres of land, much of it in prime pasture grass. A good deal of the land encircling Waimea belongs to the ranch, or did at one time, as did some of the prime oceanfront land now occupied by the plush hotels of the Kohala coast. A ranch visitor center is located in the middle of town, and the old Parker homestead is open to visitors. Admission is charged.

The drive leaves Waimea to the south on HI 190 for 6.2 miles and then forks to the left on the Saddle Road (HI 200). Almost immediately the road begins to climb through green, rolling ranch country. Ancient cinder cones,

Observatories on Mauna Kea, with Maui in the distance.

now covered with vegetation, distinguish themselves from other hills by the saucerlike depressions at their summits. As the road continues upward, sweeping views of the Kona coast unveil to the rear. After about 12 miles, the verdant fields give way to dry grasses struggling through old, disintegrating lava. The highway passes the entrance to Pohakuloa Military Camp, and if maneuvers are in progress, trucks and other large vehicles may be encountered on the road.

At Mauna Kea State Recreation Area, almost 19 miles from the HI 19/200 junction, low-cost park cabins are available by prior reservation only (see Appendix). Camping is not permitted. Vegetation virtually disappears now, as the route crosses the massive, black flows of Mauna Loa. Miles of jagged lava cover the landscape on both sides of the road as far as the eye can see. The flanks of both giant volcanoes loom on either side, their peaks beyond view at more than 13,000 feet above sea level.

Two side trips, mentioned at the beginning of this drive, are now possible. The first of these is a drive up the slopes of Mauna Kea, at 13,796 feet the highest mountain in the state and in the Pacific—easily topping Japan's Mount Fuji (12,388 feet). For those driving conventional vehicles, the trip will end at the visitor center of the Ellison Onizuka Institute for International Astronomy, 6.2 steep miles up the mountain at 9,300 feet.

The visitor center was named for a Hawaii-born astronaut who was killed in the explosion of the space shuttle *Challenger* in 1986. It is open Friday through Monday, and offers exhibits, a slide presentation, and a stargazing program. A large support center for the summit observatories is located just above the visitor center. Here, scientists and other technicians are able to sleep and eat when they are off duty, without being required to come down off the mountain, thus preserving their altitude acclimatization. A rare, high-altitude plant, the silversword, may be viewed in a nearby enclosure. This plant grows here on Mauna Loa, and at Haleakala on Maui.

Tourists with four-wheel-drive vehicles may drive the additional 6.6 miles to the summit of the mountain. Mauna Kea's last eruption took place about 3,600 years ago, and its summit crater has collapsed and eroded away. However, numerous cinder cones provide a surreal setting for the astronomic observatories. The summit of the mountain houses the world's foremost astronomical complex. As of this writing, five nations had ten instruments on Mauna Kea, and four more were planned. The largest telescope in existence, the Keck, is already functioning, and Keck II is under construction. Although it is possible to drive or walk along the roads on the summit, none of the observatories are open to the public. The University of Hawaii offers free tours of its observatory on weekends to persons providing their own four-wheel-drive transportation. Check with the Onizuka Visitor Center for details.

The drive up Mauna Kea begins at a small hunter check-in shack on the right side of HI 200, about 7 miles past Mauna Kea State Recreation Area. Directly opposite the shack, on the left, a paved road heads up the mountain. There are no signs or other markings. Snow is common on the mountain from November through March, normally above the 10,000 foot level. The road is usually kept clear, but it is not advisable to drive up the mountain if it is snowing. Average temperatures at the summit are 42 degrees in summer, and 31 degrees in winter, and the high winds that frequently buffet the mountain can make it much colder. Both warm clothing and sun protection are necessary for exploring the summit area.

The other possible side trip is an 18-mile drive up the slope of Mauna Loa to a weather observatory at 11,000 feet. The route can be driven with a conventional-drive vehicle and is paved or hard surfaced all the way. This trip is of interest for its sweeping views and to gain an appreciation of the astounding volume of lava that has flowed down the north flank of the mountain. The road to the observatory begins less than 0.5 mile past the Mauna Kea road, just beyond a large hill on the right. It is unmarked. Turning right off the highway, the narrow road proceeds for 3.8 miles to a fork at a curve. The route bears left at the fork, and continues another 4.4 miles to a sharp right turn near some antennas and other instruments. New pavement soon begins, and after an additional 9 miles, the road reaches a small parking lot just below the weather observatory. The observatory is not open to the public. The parking lot is primarily used by hikers, and a short walk down a rough jeep road leads to the trailhead. From here it is a 6-mile hike

Lake Waiau on the slopes of Mauna Kea, at 13,020 feet elevation, is the third highest lake in the United States.

over rough lava to the summit of the mountain at 13,679 feet. Weather conditions are similar to those on Mauna Kea.

Altitude sickness is possible on both these side trips, due to the rapid ascent in a short period of time. It is usually manifested by headache, mild nausea, or light-headedness. Medication, such as aspirin, may relieve this discomfort. More serious symptoms—dizziness, disorientation, or breathing difficulties—require immediate descent to lower altitude.

Following these side trips, the drive begins a winding, 25-mile descent to Hilo on HI 200. Lush vegetation replaces the stark volcanic barrenness, as the windward climate asserts itself. Fog or heavy mist can occur here as the wet windward and dry leeward breezes meet. The drive ends in the northeastern part of Hilo.

10

The Gold Coast: Opulence and Archaeology

General description: This 122-mile loop takes in sweeping coastal and mountain views, some of the most important archaeological and historical sites in the islands, and the plush, luxury resorts of Hawaii's "Gold Coast."
Special attractions: Kaloko-Honokohau National Historical Park, Kona Coast State Park, Anaehoomalu Bay, Kalahuipuaa Fishponds, Puako petroglyphs, Hapuna Beach, Puukohola Heiau National Historic Site, Lapakahi State Historical Park, Mookini Heiau, King Kamehameha Birthing Stones, Pololu Valley Lookout, hiking, backpacking, camping, swimming, snorkeling, scuba diving, surfing, sailboarding, fishing.
Location: The northwest section of the island of Hawaii.
Drive route numbers: Hawaii Highways 19, 270, 250, and 190.
Camping: Four campgrounds are located along the route: Spencer, Mahukona, Kapaa, and Keokea, all county beach parks. Permits are required.
Services: Kailua-Kona: all services (major hotels, restaurants, shopping centers, auto service and repair, etc.). Kawaihae: gas, two restaurants. Hawi: limited accommodations, gas, restaurant. Waimea: two motels, restaurants, gas, and most shopping.
Nearby attractions: Kiholo Bay, South Kohala resorts.

 The Drive

Leaving Kailua-Kona to the north on HI 19, the drive quickly reaches Kaloko-Honokohau National Historical Park. Still under development, the park contains more than four hundred archaeological sites, including ancient fishponds, several *heiau*, a *holua* (a slide built for the entertainment of Hawaiian royalty), and a section of an *alaloa* (a main road or a trail around an island) that was often referred to as the "King's Highway." This particular trail once reached from Kailua-Kona to Kawaihae. Also in the park are numerous petroglyphs, and the "Queen's Bath," a freshwater pool where Hawaiian chieftesses reputedly bathed while guards stood watch on the lava pillars still standing around the pool. Some local historians believe that the remains of Kamehameha lie buried in a secret location somewhere within the park. The visitor center for the park is temporarily located in the Kaloko Industrial Park, across the highway from the park grounds.

Returning to HI 19 and continuing north, the drive soon enters a world of lava. Mile upon mile of jagged, black crust seems to stretch endlessly from the mountains to the sea. Although it is difficult to picture any kind of development in this inhospitable environment, this is Hawaii's Gold Coast, named for the many luxury resorts that have sprung up here in recent years. Proving that where there is sun, sea, and money, anything is possible, the lava has been made to bloom. Topsoil and trees have been brought in, fields of lava pulverized, and water diverted from faraway mountain sources. Golf courses, swimming pools, and expensive hotels have sprouted, oasis fashion, where not a blade of grass grew before.

These resorts are worth a visit in themselves. The Royal Waikoloa sits on lovely, palm-lined Anaehoomalu Bay (see below). The nearby fantasyland Hilton Waikoloa Village, with a train and boats running through the lobby and water running almost everywhere else, hosts an excellent Asian art collection displayed along a landscaped corridor. The grounds of the Mauna Lani include historic fishponds that are still functional. And the newly refurbished Mauna Kea is home to the renowned Laurence Rockefeller Far Eastern art collection.

Anaehoomalu Bay is fringed by a curved, palm-lined beach.

The Gold Coast: Opulence and Archaeology

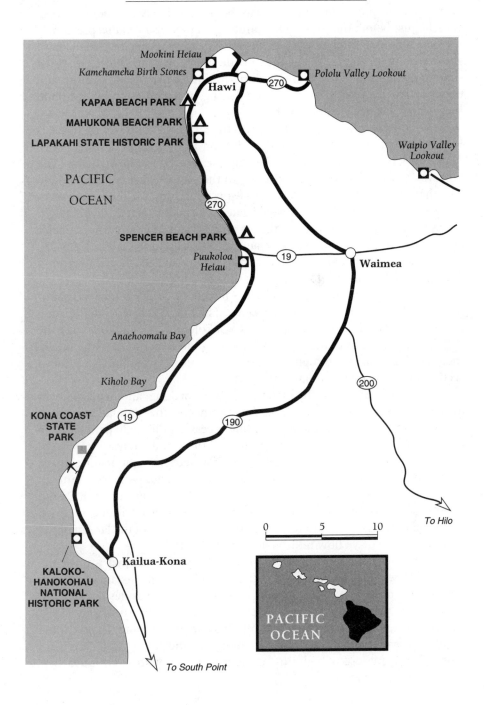

About 2.5 miles past the airport, the drive turns left on a rough, 4.3-mile-long road through a lava field to Kona Coast State Park. The road is narrow and in poor condition, but can be driven slowly in a conventional vehicle. Just before the parking lot, another section of the *alaloa* previously seen in Kaloko-Honokohau crosses the road. At the parking lot a small kiawe grove with picnic tables lies behind a wide beach. Strolling north, it is possible to combine beach walking with hiking the *alaloa*, for a beautiful and easy coastal trip past marvelous secluded beaches and a former fishpond that is now a water bird sanctuary.

Another lovely spot, 12 miles from the airport and just off the drive is Kiholo Bay, with its protected turquoise lagoon and several fresh water pools. Access to Kiholo is from a dirt road leading seaward from the highway. (The best way to find this road is by driving to the scenic overlook over Kiholo Bay, then turning *back* toward Kailua-Kona, watching for the first road to the sea, about 0.5 mile.) An unlocked gate is normally open during daylight hours, but a sign warns drivers that it may be closed at any time. A safer approach is to park before the gate and walk a mile to the coast. Here, another mile or so walk along the coast passes two very plush private homes and two beach houses before reaching the secluded lagoon.

The drive next turns off HI 19 at Anaehoomalu Bay, a curved, palm-lined beach, backed by ancient fishponds. The beach is reached by turning off the highway on the road to the Royal Waikoloan Hotel and following the "public access" signs to the the public parking lot. In addition to the beach, there is an extensive petroglyph field on the resort grounds, as well as a section of the by now familiar *alaloa*.

The drive returns to the highway by backtracking, and in a little over a mile turns seaward once again at the entrance to the Mauna Lani Hotel, following the signs to the public coastline access. At the small parking lot, a paved pathway crosses an ancient lava flow with several interesting archaeological features, including a cave used as living quarters in prehistoric times. At the coast the trail ends at the Kalahuipuaa Fishponds—ancient, but still in production. Also on the grounds of the Mauna Lani are the Puako petroglyph fields, one of the most extensive on this coast, with nearly three thousand carvings. The trail from the hotel leads to one of the largest of the groupings. The drive now returns once more to HI 19.

It is now possible to see four of the five volcanoes that formed the island of Hawaii: Hualalai to the south, Mauna Loa in the distant southeast, Mauna Kea to the east, and Kohala in the northeast. Five miles north of the Mauna Lani, Hapuna Beach State Recreation Area encompasses the widest white sand beach on the island. Two-hundred-yards-wide and 0.5 mile long, Hapuna provides swimming, body surfing, and snorkeling. But care is required during periods of high surf, as there are no lifeguards at this beach. A new luxury hotel and golf course now occupy the north end of the beach. The entrance to the Mauna Kea Beach Hotel is a mile past Hapuna.

Just south of Kawaihae (1 mile past the Mauna Kea entrance), HI 19 turns right and uphill. The drive continues straight, however, along the coast on what is now HI 270, toward Kawaihae and Hawi. It soon reaches *Puukohola Heiau* National Historic Site, one of the most important *heiau* in Hawaiian history. Overlooking Kawaihae Bay, it was built by Kamehameha in 1791, when he was at war with other chiefs of the Big Island. Kamehameha was told by a *kahuna*, or priest, that if he built a *heiau* at this spot he would become ruler of all the Hawaiian Islands.

As the *heiau* was being completed, Kamehameha invited his chief rival to the site to discuss peace. In an act of open treachery, Kamehameha had the arriving chief killed, and sacrificed his body to consecrate the *heiau*. Nineteen years and many battles later, the prophecy was finally fulfilled. In addition to visiting the *heiau*, you can stop at nearby Spencer Beach County Park which has a fine beach, restrooms, tennis courts, and a campground.

North from Kawaihae, the drive follows miles of dry, uninhabited coastline, where parched grasses and *kiawe* trees meet the rocky coast and the cobalt blue sea. Scuba divers frequent this wind-protected coast for its dramatic dropoffs and big game fish. Twelve miles from Puukohola, Lapakahi

Spencer Beach Park, an attractive location near Puu Kohola Heiau, allows camping.

State Historical Park preserves the site of an abandoned fishing village. Although hard to imagine, a settlement prospered in this harsh place for five hundred years. A self-guiding trail brochure is available, with a map keyed to various archaeological remains, but it takes a good deal of imagination to visualize the village from what is left. A short distance north of Lapakahi, Mahukona and Kapaa Beach county parks offer waterfront campgrounds.

The drive next leaves HI 270 at a sign for Upolu Airport, about 7 miles past Lapakahi. Just before reaching the airfield, it turns left again onto a narrow dirt road paralleling the shore for about 2 miles. A large stone wall appears on a rise to the left. This is Mookini *Heiau*, built in 480 A. D. and used exclusively by Hawaii's kings and ruling chiefs for worship and human sacrifice. Most *heiau* were constructed atop a huge stone platform (such as the one at Puukohola), but Mookini is a walled enclosure nearly as large as a football field. According to legend, it was built in one night from stones passed hand-to-hand from Pololu Valley, more than 10 miles away—a feat that would have required fifteen thousand to eighteen thousand men to perform.

Continuing along the dirt road 0.5 mile past Mookini, a fence encloses the spot where Kamehameha was reportedly born. The large rocks within the enclosure are said to be his birthing stones. The drive now reverses

*The wild, uninhabited northeastern Kohala coast, as seen from the
end of the road at Pololu Valley.*

direction and returns to HI 270, passing through the small towns of Hawi and Kapaau, where a statue of Kamehameha stands. In the late 1870s the city of Honolulu commissioned a statue of the king from a sculptor in Florence, Italy. When the ship bringing the statue to Hawaii sank on a reef, a duplicate was ordered, which now stands in the famous square opposite the Iolani Palace in Honolulu. Later, the original statue was recovered from the wreck, and placed here in Kapaau, commemorating the king's birth nearby.

Seven miles of quiet, rural scenery lead from Kapaau to Pololu Valley Lookout. A mile before the lookout a side road leads to Keokea Beach County Park, a quiet location with an attractive campground. HI 270 ends at the lookout, which affords a dramatic view of the windward Kohala coast. Pololu is the northernmost of seven beautiful, isolated valleys along this shore, separated by high seacliffs. Only Waipio, the southernmost, is inhabited. A path leading to the bottom of Pololu Valley takes about fifteen to twenty minutes to descend. The gray sand beach is good for a stroll or a swim if the water is calm.

The drive returns to Hawi on HI 270, turning left on HI 250 (Kohala Mountain Road) for a 20-mile trip to Waimea. It now climbs through the foothills of Kohala Mountain, the oldest of the five volcanoes that formed the island of Hawaii, and the only one considered extinct. Spectacular, sweeping views of the Kona coast appear as the route winds over rolling, green ranch country. HI 250 ends in Waimea, the headquarters of the Parker Ranch (see Scenic Drive 9).

In the center of town, the drive turns right on HI 190, which roughly parallels the coast highway (HI 19), but inland and at a higher elevation. And the scenery is a distinct change from the stark, black lava fields encountered on the coast highway at the beginning of the trip. Leaving Waimea, ranch country predominates, with grass covered cinder cones on the left and broad expanses to the sea on the right. Six miles south of Waimea, Hawaii 200 joins from the left; the juncture is marked by a large, partially open cinder cone now covered in grass.

Over the next 14 miles the land gradually becomes less suitable for ranching, as rock and lava begin to outcrop in the fields. At Puuanahulu, a few houses perch high for fine views over the cluster of green volcanic hills to the south. The dominant feature is now Hualalai, its slopes blanketing the view on the left, and its lava flows marching to the sea on the right. About 10 miles from Puuanahulu the road begins to descend to Kailua-Kona, and once again, lush vegetation overwhelms the black lava, continuing until just before the town and the end of the drive.

11

Coffee Country, South Point, and the Ka'u Coast

General description: This 120-mile drive circles the southern half of Mauna Loa, the world's largest mountain mass. It passes through Kona Coffee country and macadamia nut orchards, crosses Mauna Loa's massive southwest lava flows, visits windy and historic South Point (the southernmost location in the United States), rounds the point to the island's southeast coast, and ends at Hawaii Volcanoes National Park.

Special attractions: Kahaluu Beach Park, Kealakekua Bay, Puuhonua O Honaunau National Historic Park, Manuka State Wayside, Road to the Sea, South Point, Punaluu Black Sand Beach, hiking, camping, swimming, snorkeling, scuba diving, surfing, fishing.

Location: The south coast of the island of Hawaii.

Drive route numbers: Alii Drive, Hawaii Highway 11, South Point Road.

Camping: Six campgrounds are located along the route: Hookena, Milolii, Whittington, and Punaluu Beach County parks, Manuka State Park, and Namakani Piao in the national park. All but the latter require permits.

Services: Kailua-Kona: all services (major hotels, restaurants, shopping centers, auto service and repair, etc.). Captain Cook: 1 small hotel, 2 restaurants, gas, limited shopping. Naalehu: 1 small motel, snack bar, gas, limited shopping.

Nearby attractions: Green Sand Beach, Milolii fishing village.

 The Drive

Starting at the King Kamehameha Hotel, the drive leaves Kailua-Kona southward along Alii Drive. The route initially follows the coastline, passing oceanfront homes, condominiums, and two beach parks, White Sands and Kahaluu. The latter, 4.5 miles from the hotel, is famous for the great number and variety of tropical fish that can be seen in shallow water close to shore. Even green sea turtles swim by, surprisingly undisturbed by the crowd of snorkelers. The snorkeling is so unusual and easy here that it is worth a stop. You can rent masks, snorkels, and fins for a reasonable rate right on the beach.

At Keauhou, the road curves sharply to the left and climbs to an intersection with HI 11. Turning right, the road continues a gradual climb to

Coffee Country, South Point, and the Ka'u Coast

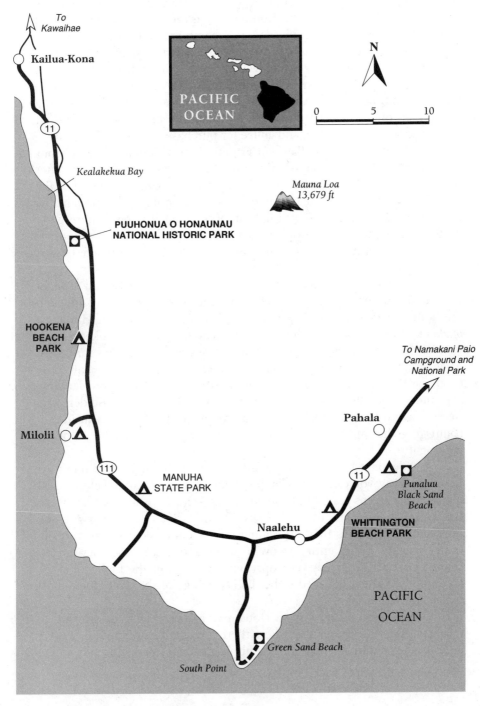

about 1,500 feet, leaving the shoreline far below, filling the west with a forever view of the blue Pacific. This is Kona Coffee country. The elevation, abundant sunshine, and misty rain provide an ideal climate for growing this gourmet brew. Until recently, the Kona coast was the only place in the United States where coffee was grown. Now it is being grown on all the main islands of Hawaii but Lanai, and it may soon be growing there.

Ten miles from Kailua-Kona the drive passes through the small towns of Kealakekua and Captain Cook and then leaves the highway at a right fork, descending steeply to Kealakekua Bay. The road to the bay passes a coffee mill, one of several that process the locally grown Kona coffee. It offers free tours, free coffee, and coffee for purchase.

It was at Kealakekua Bay that Captain James Cook dropped anchor and came ashore on the Big Island for the first time in January 1779, after discovering the islands in January of the previous year. At the end of the road, fronting the bay, is the *Hikiau Heiau*, where Cook was honored by the local chiefs. Less than a month later he was killed leading a shore party trying to secure return of a stolen boat. A white obelisk to Cook's memory is across the bay on its northern shore, not far from the spot where he was killed.

Rather than return to HI 11 from the *heiau,* you can continue straight (south) on the narrow paved road across the lava fields for 3.8 miles to Puuhonua O Honaunau National Historical Park. In ancient Hawaii, a *puuhonua* was a "place of refuge," where persons who had broken a *kapu* (one of the strict rules regulating Hawaiian society) could find sanctuary. After certain rituals, the *kapu*-breaker was free to leave without penalty. The 6-acre park contains a mausoleum, a *heiau* site, tide pools, a canoe landing, and interpretive displays. A small admission is charged, and Golden Age/Access Passports are honored. An attractive picnic area in an oceanside coconut grove lies at the end of a dirt road leading from the left end of the parking lot.

A wide, paved road leads 3.6 miles uphill from the park to rejoin HI 11. On the way, you can stop at Saint Benedict's, a small painted church just off the park's access road. For the next 15 miles the drive alternates between forests, ranch land, and old lava flows, the sea far below on the right, and the seemingly endless flank of Mauna Loa reaching skyward on the left. Coffee has given way entirely now to ranchland and macadamia nut orchards. One of the extensive properties upland from the highway is the McCandless Ranch, believed to be the last refuge of the *alala*, the almost extinct Hawaiian crow.

Continuing 2.5 miles from Honaunau a side road leads seaward to Hookena Beach County Park, where there is a small campground. Twelve miles farther, a narrow road on the right leads to an interesting side trip to the fishing village of Milolii. Descending steeply to the coast, the road skirts an ominous black lava flow that forced relocation of the town to its present site. This small collection of modest houses is the last functioning fishing village in the state. A close-knit community of mostly Hawaiian ancestry, Milolii still follows a way of life established by preceding generations. There are no shops, restaurants, hotels, or tourists. Nor are there any grass shacks and hula skirts—just simple, wooden houses, and residents in jeans and T-shirts engaged in their day-to-day activities. There is a campground at Milolii Beach County Park, just outside the village. It is a small park, usually crowded with resident activities.

Returning to HI 11 by the same route, the drive soon reaches Manuka State Park, where camping is allowed in a three-sided rock shelter with a roof. A 3.5-mile-loop hiking trail leads from the picnic area, up through an *ohia* forest to a collapsed lava tube, now filled with vegetation. The *ohia* is the most common native Hawaiian tree and one of the first plants to grow back on new lava fields.

A little less than 2 miles past Manuka, a cinder road turns off to the right. This is the Road to the Sea, one of the few accesses to this wild, deserted shoreline, where cinder cones, tidal pools, and green sand beaches lie in total isolation. By proceeding slowly, a conventional-drive vehicle can normally drive all but the last section of this road. However, if the road

Temple and tiki at Puuhonua O Honaunau.

81

appears too rough at any point, it is best to stop and continue on foot.

The route returns the way it came, and once back on HI 11 it begins to cross wide, massive lava flows on both sides of the highway, sprawling from the sea to high up the slopes of Mauna Loa. Surprisingly, scattered houses appear in this devastated landscape, indications of several of the largest and most controversial land development schemes in the state. These developments, carved checkerboard fashion out of the 1907 lava flows, cover more than 30 square miles.

Originally, these lots were offered for sale to mainland prospects unwise enough to buy a piece of "paradise" sight unseen. Operating for more than twenty years, these developments are still only sparsely inhabited. Periodically, the county offers tax lien sales of hundreds of these lots, abandoned by their discouraged purchasers. On-site offices still offer 3-acre and larger lots for sale, now to buyers who can see what they are getting. Most of the lots are without utilities or other improvements, and all are under the volcano's somber eye. Although there hasn't been an eruption in this direction since 1950, Mauna Loa is the most unpredictable and potentially dangerous of Hawaii's two active volcanoes.

As the road approaches the southern end of the island, the lava fields gradually give way to fertile soil and vegetation is more abundant. The turnoff to South Point appears on the right, 11.6 miles past the Road to the Sea

The Road to the Sea, one of the few accesses to the isolated south Kona shoreline.

Diamond Head Peak, Oahu (Drive 1)
ALL COLOR PHOTOGRAPHY BY ANN CECIL

Hanauma Bay, Oahu (Drive 1)

Early morning in "Sherwood Forest," Waimanalo State Recreation Area, Oahu (Drive 1)

Snorkeling at Lumahai Beach, north shore of Kauai (Drive 12)

Pink plumerias

Kalalau Valley Overlook, Kauai (Drive 14)

Hikers resting on the edge of Haleakala Crater, Maui (Drive 4)

Naue Stream, Hamakua Coast, Hawaii (Drive 9)

Hibiscus

Hana Coastline, Maui (Drive 5)

Hawaiian dancers in Honolulu, Oahu

Garden of the Gods, Lanai (Drive 18)

Lava flow at Volcano National Park, Hawaii (Drive 8)

The Iao Needle, Hawaii (Drive 6)

intersection. The road is bumpy and narrow but fully paved. Windmills churning to produce electricity, billowing waves of grass, and trees bending almost to the ground attest to the stiff winds that sweep across this sparsely inhabited landscape.

South Point is the southernmost point in the United States. Called *Ka Lae* by the Hawaiians, it is an area of considerable archaeological importance. One of the most interesting finds is a series of circular holes drilled in the rocks by ancient fishermen, who used them as tie-downs for their canoes. Thus securely anchored to shore, the canoes could drift safely in rich fishing grounds swept by strong currents and winds. Modern day fishermen employ the same technique by winching their boats out from the moorings visible at the base of the steep cliffs.

At the very end of the point, about 11 miles from HI 11, a jeep road leads from the parking lot 3 miles northeast to Green Sand Beach, a popular destination for hikers or four-wheel-drivers. The color of the beach comes from olivine crystals washing out of a shoreline cone. The cone, now about half eroded, has formed an attractive, curved beach. There is no fresh water or shade in the area, and if one chooses to swim, swim with caution and only on calm days.

Returning to HI 11 from South Point, the drive continues east for 8 miles to Naalehu, the southernmost town in the United States. With the move from the leeward to the windward side of the island, the change in landscape is dramatic. Gone are all traces of lava fields. Lush green hills and pastures thick with rich grass drop to a deep blue sea. Tropical trees and plants abound.

Three miles past the town, Whittington Beach County Park offers an attractive campground. A group of high hills and plateaus appear to the right, 3 to 5 miles distant from the highway. The large, symmetrical cinder cone is Puu One, 3,220 feet high.

The turnoff to Punaluu Black Sand Beach lies 5 miles past Whittington. Located at the north end of the Seamountain Resort, Punaluu's palm-lined sands and freshwater pond make it the most attractive of the island's black sand beaches. Camping is permitted at the beach park, which is usually crowded with visitors and local people.

In the remaining 30 miles to Hawaii Volcanoes National Park, the road will climb slowly from sea level to 4,000 feet. Mauna Loa, now on the left, soon dominates the entire left side of the road. Although much more of the mountain is visible on this side of the island, its true summit remains hidden from view. Until 1996, this area was the province of Ka'u Sugar Company; cane fields stretched from Naalehu almost to the border of the national park. The plantation has now closed, leaving the town of Pahala and several settlement camps high and dry. North of the turnoff to Pahala more macadamia nut orchards appear.

Pavilion behind fresh water pond at Punaluu Black Sand Beach.

As the drive approaches the park, the volcano begins to assert itself. Old, disintegrated lava flows replace soil, and vegetation thins out. Soon scrub, thin tufts of grass, and stunted *ohia* trees are all that grow. Two miles before the park entrance, Namakani Paio offers camping in an attractive setting with no fee or reservations required. Cabins may also be rented here through the Volcano House Hotel, opposite from the park visitor center. The town of Volcano, 1 mile east of the park entrance, offers limited accommodations, some shopping, limited-hours restaurants, and gas. For a tour of the national park see Scenic Drive 8.

KAUAI

Kauai is the fourth largest of the main islands and is the oldest geologically, between 3.8 and 5.6 million years old. When Captain James Cook discovered the Hawaiian Islands for the western world in January 1778, he came ashore at Waimea, Kauai. But when he returned the following year, he made landfall on the southernmost islands in the chain; his successors tended to follow in his wake. Kauai's distance from the main islands of Hawaii has, until recent times, kept it insulated to some extent from its neighbors. Even Kamehameha, who united all the islands under his control, was unable to conquer Kauai. It was the last to come under his power, and did so by peaceful negotiation.

Many people regard Kauai as the most beautiful of all the Hawaiian Islands. Its lush beauty is often attributed to the additional rainfall Kaui receives compared to the other islands, and this has led to the erroneous impression that Kauai is rainy. It isn't. Although Mount Waialeale is one of the wettest spots in the world, rainfall in most parts of Kauai compares favorably with similar sections of other islands. The island has been hit hard in recent times, however, by two devastating hurricanes, Iwa in 1982 and Iniki in 1992. The latest calamity destroyed over one thousand homes, closed every hotel on the island (some have still not reopened as of the date of this writing), interrupted power and phone service for weeks, and caused almost $2 billion in damage. But nature and man have both responded quickly, and the island has mostly recovered. Kauai remains probably the most scenically attractive of all the islands.

Area: 558 square miles
Population: 54,000
Airports: Lihue.
Rental car offices: Lihue Airport.

12

The Eastern and Northern Shores to the Na Pali Coast

General description: Starting in Lihue, this 52-mile drive visits two waterfalls, passes 9 county beach parks, and reveals some of the most magnificent coastal scenery found anywhere in the world. Two water-filled caves can be explored, one directly along the highway. The route continues to the end of the highway at Kee Beach, and the beginning of Kauai's incomparable Na Pali Coast.

Special attractions: Wailua Falls, Opaekaa Falls, Sleeping Giant, Royal Coconut Grove, Hole in the Mountain, Kilauea Point, Hanalei Valley Lookout, Hanalei Bay, Mission Houses, Lumahai Beach, Wet Caves, Kee Beach, Na Pali Coast Trail, hiking, backpacking, camping, swimming, snorkeling, scuba diving, sailboarding, kayaking.

Location: Eastern side of the island of Kauai.

Drive route numbers: Hawaii Highway 56 (Kuhio Highway).

Camping: One private and five public campgrounds are along the route: Hanamaulu, Anahola, Anini, Hanalei, and Haena are all county beach parks, and Camp Naue is operated by the YMCA. Permits are required, and camping at Hanalei is only permitted on weekends and holidays.

Services: Lihue: all services (major hotels, restaurants, shopping centers, auto service and repair, etc.). Kapaa: major hotels, restaurants, shopping centers, gas. Princeville/Hanalei: major hotels, restaurants, shopping centers, gas.

Nearby attractions: Fern Grotto, Hanakapiai Beach, Hanakapiai Falls.

 ## The Drive

Driving north from Lihue (population 5,500) on Hawaii Highway 56 (HI 56), you will turn left on HI 583 and travel 3 miles to Wailua Falls. Here, the South Fork of the Wailua River plunges 80 feet to a large, circular pool, and then flows to the sea. Returning to HI 56, less than a mile farther north on the right side, Hanamaulu Road leads to a large, attractive campground at Hanamaulu Beach Park with modern facilities.

After another 4 miles the drive crosses the Wailua River, the only navigable river in Hawaii. Before the bridge, a turnoff to the left leads to the Wailua Marina, where boats ply the river to the Fern Grotto, a riverside cave

The Eastern and Northern Shores to the Na Pali Coast

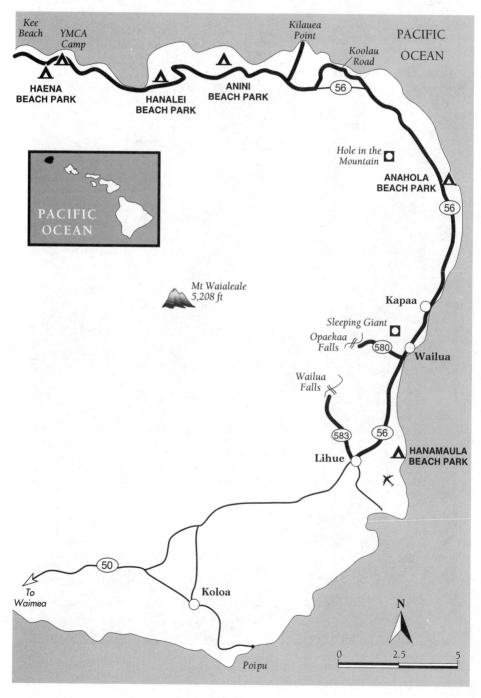

Kee Beach

YMCA Camp

HAENA BEACH PARK

HANALEI BEACH PARK

ANINI BEACH PARK

Kilauea Point

Koolau Road

PACIFIC OCEAN

56

PACIFIC OCEAN

Hole in the Mountain

ANAHOLA BEACH PARK

56

Mt Waialeale 5,208 ft

Kapaa

Sleeping Giant

Opaekaa Falls

580

Wailua

Wailua Falls

583

56

Lihue

HANAMAULA BEACH PARK

50

To Waimea

Koloa

Poipu

N

0   2.5   5

Wailua Falls.

with hundreds of ferns sprouting from its ceiling and walls. Once across the river, the drive leaves the highway again, turns left on Route 580 and proceeds 3 miles to Opaekaa Falls, a 40-foot drop of the North Fork of the Wailua River. Across the road from the parking lot is a good view over the main Wailua River and boats en route to the Fern Grotto. The drive then retraces HI 580 back to HI 56.

The towns of Wailua (population 2,000) and Kapaa (8,000) are mainly noted for hotels, shopping, and restaurants, but the area still retains its scenic quality. The Royal Coconut Grove, now bordered by a large, tourist-oriented shopping center, reaches to the edge of the highway just north of Wailua. Between Wailua and Kapaa the Sleeping Giant comes into view on the left. When seen from the highway, Nounou Mountain, a low ridgeline to the east, resembles a reclining man.

Just past the town of Anahola, 7.5 miles from Wailua, a right turn leads to a campground at Anahola County Beach Park. The bay is also a well-known surfing spot. Just north of town, the Anahola Mountains loom above the highway on the west side. Observant travelers will be able to pick out the Hole in the Mountain, a natural aperture in the rock that allows light to shine through from one side of the ridgeline to the other. Legend claims an angry giant threw his spear through the mountain at that point.

About 12 miles north of the Wailua River bridge, the drive once more leaves the highway and turns right on Koolau Road, for a short tour through the lush, rural Hawaii that tourists rarely see. A side trip here leads to lovely Moloaa Bay.

At the town of Kilauea, 3.5 miles past the point where Koolau Road returns to HI 56, the drive leaves the highway once more, turning right and through the town for a 2-mile trip to Kilauea Point, a seabird sanctuary. The tall lighthouse here houses the world's largest "clamshell lens," which has now been replaced by a small high-intensity light. The extensive view of the coastline and of hundreds of birds flying and roosting on the sea cliffs and the islands offshore is worth the small admission charge.

Returning to HI 56 you will continue to Anini Beach County Park, a quiet, modern campground on a beautiful, wooded beach, 2.5 miles farther down the highway. Turn right on the second Kalihiwai Road. Anini also offers good snorkeling and is one of the most popular sailboarding locations on Kauai.

Just past the large hotel and condominium complex of Princeville is the pullout for Hanalei Valley Lookout. If it is raining in the mountains, long ribbons of water cascade more than 1,000 feet to the valley below. The green taro paddies stretching along the Hanalei River also serve as a water bird sanctuary. Hanalei Garden Farms, north of the highway after crossing the river, maintains a herd of bison (the only Great Plains "buffalo" in the state). They are often visible from the road.

Taro fields in Hanalei Valley.

Hanalei (population 500) offers a few restaurants, a small shopping center, and a marvelous, world-renowned bay. Up to a hundred sailboats may be at anchor in the bay during the summer, but winter's waves and winds drive them all away. The town is also the focal point for boat tours of the incomparable Na Pali coast. A beach campground on the bay is only open on weekends, and offers the usual amenities. The Mission Houses at the far end of the town differ from most of the homes built by the first missionaries to Hawaii, incorporating Polynesian rather than New England architecture in their construction.

After Hanalei, it is only 7 miles to the end of the road at Kee Beach, but it is an incredibly scenic 7 miles. Crossing two one-lane wooden bridges, the drive enters a place a world apart from the rest of the island. Traffic drops off sharply, the few homes are widely spaced, and small dirt roads disappear into high-walled valleys choked with tropical vegetation. Breathtaking small bays and beaches follow one after the other. This is Bali Hai, somewhere in the remote South Pacific, not part of the United States at all. In fact, Lumahai, one of the most beautiful of the beaches, was the setting for the film of *South Pacific*, one of the first of many films to be made on Kauai.

Haena Beach County Park, with a cave on the opposite side of the road, offers picnicking and camping in an attractive setting, but with run-down facilities. A popular snorkeling and scuba site known locally as "Tunnels," lies a few hundred yards east of Haena. The Waikapalae Wet Cave, a short hike from a parking lot, is a large lava tube, partially filled with fresh water. Swimming is possible in this eerie chamber, and in the Waikanaloa Wet Cave less than 0.5 mile farther down the highway.

The drive ends at Kee Beach, where a small swimming lagoon is protected by an offshore reef. The platform in the rocks to the left of the beach is an ancient hula site. Nearby are the ruins of a *heiau* dedicated to *Laka*, the goddess of the hula. On important occasions in ancient times, Hawaiians threw blazing firebrands from the high cliff behind the beach. Until some years ago, the practice was commemorated by pushing the flaming embers of a huge bonfire off the cliff on the 4th of July.

The parking lot at Kee is also the start of the Na Pali Coast Trail (Kalalau Trail). This 11-mile ancient pathway once connected the Hawaiian valley communities of the north shore, now abandoned by their former inhabitants. Today, it provides the most spectacular hike in the islands. Even a short, twenty-minute walk up the trail reveals the awesome splendor of the Na Pali Coast. A longer hike (2.5 hours round-trip) reaches Hanakapiai Beach, a wonderful white sand oasis in a jungle-like setting. The walk should not be made in street shoes or beach thongs; hiking boots or jogging shoes are appropriate. Arrangements can also be made in Hanalei to see this entire magnificent coast by boat.

Mission House in Hanalei.

13

The South Shore to Poipu Beach, and West to Polihale

General description: From Lihue, this 45-mile drive visits the Menehune Fishpond and proceeds west to Poipu Beach. It then continues west through the small sugar towns of the south shore, until reaching Polihale State Park, the western end of the famed Na Pali Coast. Six beach parks are located along the route.

Special attractions: Menehune Fishpond, Poipu Beach, Spouting Horn, Russian Fort, Barking Sands, Polihale State Park, camping, swimming, surfing, sailboarding, snorkeling, scuba diving.

Location: On the south and west shores of the island of Kauai.

Drive route numbers: Hawaii Highways 50, 52, and 53.

Camping: Three county campgrounds and one state park are located along the drive: Niumalu, Salt Pond, and Lucy Wright County Beach Parks, and Polihale State Park. Permits are required.

Services: Lihue: all services (major hotels, restaurants, shopping centers, auto service and repair, etc.). Poipu/Koloa: major hotels, restaurants, shopping, gas. Some gas, food shopping, and restaurants are available along the route.

Nearby attractions: Waimea Canyon, Kokee State Park, Kalalau Lookout, Alakai Swamp (see Scenic Drive 14).

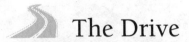

The Drive

The drive begins on Rice Street in Lihue and heads southeast toward Nawiliwili Harbor. It turns off on Waapa Road, which curves around to the right to Hulemalu Road, passes the campground at Niumalu Beach County Park, and reaches an overlook of the Alakoko Fishpond. One of the largest and best preserved in the islands, it is popularly called the Menehune Fishpond, named for the mythical race of little people who supposedly built it. Legend says the menehune lived in Hawaii prior to the arrival of the Polynesians. The menehune make a nice story, like the leprechauns of Ireland.

Continuing past the fishpond, Hulemalu Road joins Hawaii Highway 50, where the drive turns left. Sugar cane fields line both sides of the road, reaching to the foothills of the mountains—the Hoary Head range on the

The South Shore to Poipu Beach, and West to Polihale

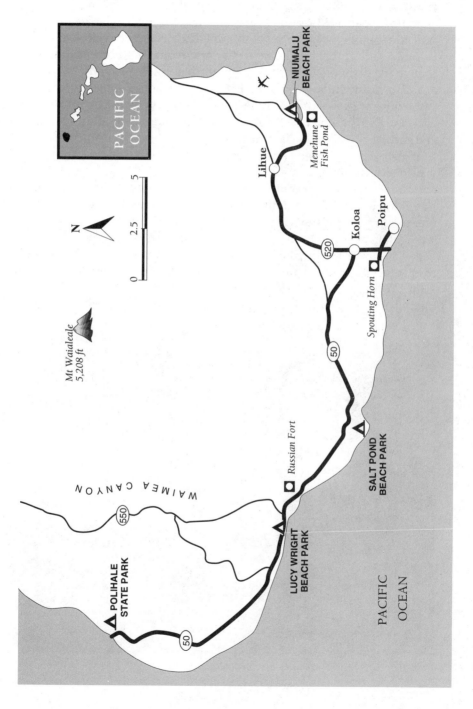

left and the slopes of Kilohana Crater on the right. The route continues west for about 5 miles, then turns south to Poipu Beach (6 miles). Prior to Hurricane Iniki in 1992, a "tree tunnel" covered much of this road. The trees were badly damaged by the hurricane, and although they are recovering well, the tunnel will take years to grow back completely. Koloa, the first town after the tunnel, is home to the first sugar mill built in Hawaii. Although the plantation closed in 1996, the old mill still stands.

Hurricane Imiki devastated Poipu and its hotels and condominiums. Although the area is back in business, two of its major hotels were still closed in 1997. Poipu Beach Park offers picnicking, swimming, snorkeling, and surfing. To reach the Spouting Horn, a large blowhole, take the first left turn after leaving Poipu, en route back to Koloa. The drive returns to HI 50 via Koloa and HI 53.

Sugar continues to dominate the landscape between the towns all the way from the sea to the mountains in the north. Acres of cane waving in the breeze surround the towns of Kalaheo, Eleele, and Hanapepe. About 2 miles west of Kalaheo, a lookout on the right reveals a dramatic view of Hanapepe Valley. Just after leaving the lookout you can see the privately owned island of Niihau. Purchased by the Sinclair family in 1864 from King Kamehameha V for $10,000 (sold to the Robinson family soon thereafter), the 70-square-mile island has remained closed to visitors ever since. A small population of

Poipu Coast.

94

Spouting Horn.

mainly ethnic Hawaiians lives on the island, engaged primarily in ranching and fishing.

It is now possible to take a helicopter tour of the island, landing for a short stop at an isolated location; however, there is no contact with the inhabitants. Coincidentally, it was also a member of the Robinson family who was the first to own the private island of Lanai, now owned by the Dole Company.

After crossing the bridge in Hanapepe, a road to the left leads to Salt Pond Beach County Park. You will find a spacious campground here. Adjacent to the beach park, ancient salt ponds still provide salt by evaporation of sea water. Only certain Hawaiian families with long-standing rights may mine the salt from this area.

Five miles from Hanapepe, just before the town of Waimea, the ruins of Fort Elizabeth stand as mute evidence of czarist Russia's attempt at Pacific expansion in the nineteenth century. Little more than rock walls remain of the fort, built by a Russian naval officer in 1815. Across the river, Waimea (population 1,800), is where Captain James Cook came ashore in January 1778, the first westerner ever to set foot in the Hawaiian Islands. The famed explorer was en route from Tahiti in search of the elusive Northwest Passage across North America, when he sighted Oahu and Kauai. He returned early the following year to winter in what he named the Sandwich Islands and found the southern islands in the chain. A statue of the great navigator stands in a small park near the center of town, just east of the Big Save store. Lucy Wright Beach County Park offers camping facilities with restrooms, showers, a small pavilion, and drinking water.

Leaving Waimea, the drive parallels a white sand beach, which stretches 15 miles from Waimea to Polihale and is one of the longest in the state. Two roads lead off the highway to Waimea Canyon (The Grand Canyon of the Pacific, see Scenic Drive 14). Miles of sugar cane border the route on both sides of the road, interspersed with occasional grazing lands for horses and cattle. After passing Barking Sands Pacific Missile Range Facility, the drive turns toward the mountains, and then becomes a dirt road through the cane fields. The drive ends at Polihale State Park, one of Hawaii's widest and longest white sand beaches, dramatically framed by the high ridges of the Na Pali Coast. You will find an excellent, modern campground here in a dramatic, isolated setting.

14

Waimea Canyon, Kokee State Park, and Kalalau Valley Overlook

General description: This 40-mile round-trip drive follows the western rim of Waimea Canyon from sea level beaches to the rain forests of Kokee State Park at an elevation of 4,000 feet.

Special attractions: Waimea Canyon, Kalalau Valley Lookout, Na Pali Coast overlooks, Kokee State Park, Kokee Natural History Museum, hiking, backpacking, fishing, camping.

Location: The western side of the island of Kauai.

Drive route number: Hawaii Highway 550.

Camping: Lucy Wright Beach County Park is located in Waimea at the beginning of the drive. A state park campground and cabins are located at Kokee. Permits are required.

Services: Waimea: gas and food shopping. There are no services along the route except the park cabins and a limited-hours snack bar at Kokee State Park.

Nearby attractions: Russian Fort, Captain Cook monument, Barking Sands, Polihale Beach, Salt Pond Beach Park.

 The Drive

Beginning in the small town of Waimea, this drive follows the entire length of Waimea Canyon, passes through the tall, dense forests of Kokee State Park, and ends on the edge of spectacular cliffs overlooking Kauai's magnificent and remote Na Pali Coast.

Waimea Canyon is often referred to as the "Grand Canyon of the Pacific." Although, at 12 miles long and 3,000 feet deep, Waimea is dwarfed by its famous Arizona cousin, the resemblance is striking. This is not surprising, since both canyons were created by erosion. But the Waimea River has had less than five million years to make its mark, while the mighty Colorado has had well over a billion. Nor will the Waimea be allowed to catch up, as the geological destiny of the Hawaiian Islands is to eventually subside back into the sea.

Waimea, population 1,700, is of little interest to travelers except as the last place to gas up and buy supplies before the trip up the canyon. This is sugar cane country, and miles of cane fields stretch along the coast north and west of the town. The cane is watered by an an extensive irrigation system, which has significantly reduced the flow of the Waimea River. A statue of Captain James Cook stands in Waimea, near the spot where the great Pacific explorer first came ashore in the Hawaiian Islands in January 1778 (see Scenic Drive 13).

Weather along the route is usually fine, although it can be cloudy or rainy at the higher elevations. The canyon receives a modest 30 to 40 inches of rain per year, and prickly pear cactus grows there. Paradoxically, only 8 miles away lies Mount Waialeale, one of the wettest spots on earth, with an annual rainfall of more than 450 inches. A noonday mist sometimes gathers along the upper reaches of the drive, blanketing otherwise spectacular views over the canyon and the Na Pali coast. For this reason, it is best to start early.

The road hugs the rim of the canyon from the beginning of the drive to its headwall, affording numerous impressive views as the canyon unfolds in depth and scope. It is a paved, two-lane road all the way, winding and steep in places, but not dangerous. Care should be taken to stay well to the right when rounding curves, and low gears are required on the descent.

The drive begins by turning right off HI 50 (coming from Lihue) onto Waimea Canyon Road, two blocks west of the small shopping center on the right side of the highway. There is a church at the corner where the turn is made. After passing a string of houses, the road begins a steep climb, and the lower end of the canyon comes into view. The road does not leave the canyon from this point on, although it is not always visible. Over the next few miles many opportunities exist to pull off the road and watch the canyon unfold. About 6 miles from the start, another road joins from the left, leading back down to Kekaha. This road may be taken on the return.

About 2 miles from the intersection a sign on the right points out the Kukui Trail. There is a wide pullout for vehicles here, and it is well worth a stop. The Iliau Nature Trail begins a short distance from the road and makes an interesting loop on the canyon rim. The Kukui is a steep foot trail descending 2.5 miles to the canyon floor. A small picnic pavilion is at the trailhead, and a short walk down the trail provides an excellent place to take photos of the canyon or to just enjoy the sweeping view.

Two miles past the Kukui pullout, Waimea Canyon Lookout is the first and best of the two official turnouts to view the canyon. It is from here that it most resembles the Grand Canyon. Layered cliffs and eroded towers loom across the chasm, and the Waimea River snakes its way through the gorge 3,000 feet below. You can often see goats grazing on the precarious ledges of the canyon wall or hear them bleating in the distance.

Returning to Waimea Canyon Road, you will see additional glimpses and flashes of the canyon without warning as the drive climbs. Watch for a

Waimea Canyon, Kokee State Park, and Kalalau Valley Overlook

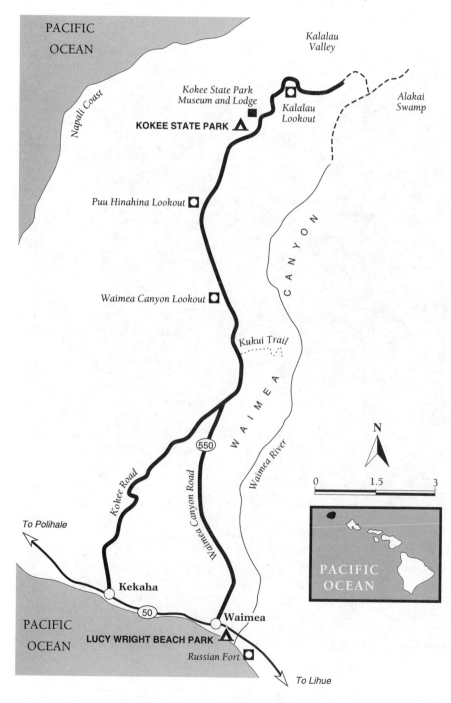

Waimea Canyon.

small sign marked Waipoo Falls, where a distant stream drops over the rim of the canyon to the floor below. Puu Hinahina, 3.5 miles from the previous overlook, is the second official lookout over the canyon. Here also is Niihau Lookout, providing a good view of this private island and its smaller sister, Lehua (see Scenic Drive 13).

After Puu Hinahina, the drive flattens and straightens somewhat, and enters Kokee State Park. The park's 4,345 acres of upland forest stand in sharp contrast to seashore Hawaii. The landscape is more reminiscent of northern California than Polynesia. Redwoods, eucalyptus, and tall pines form large groves that provide important habitat for endangered native birds. More than 35 miles of hiking trails wind through forests, meadows, and along dramatic ridges overlooking the ocean and the spectacular Na Pali cliffs. Most of the park lies at an elevation of 4,000 feet, the average temperature is 60°F, and nights can be cool.

Kokee Lodge and Kokee Natural History Museum sit in a large grassy meadow 2.5 miles past Puu Hinahina, surrounded by thick forest. The ranger station, the campground, and the park cabins are also here. The lodge offers a snack bar (limited hours) and a gift shop. The museum houses displays of area flora and fauna and offers maps and booklets for sale. Admission is free.

Surrounding the lodge and the museum, a resident rooster and chicken

Nene, *the Hawaiian state bird, at the Kalalau Lookout parking lot.*

population busily cadges food from tourists. These are not barnyard chickens but "jungle fowl," ancestors of birds brought to the islands by the original Polynesian settlers more than a thousand years ago. Escaping from domestication, they have survived in the wild only on Kauai, where the mongoose (destroyer of ground-nesting birds) was never introduced. Although the fowl at the lodge appear to be opting for civilization again, most of them still reside deep in the forest, where their crowing can be heard on the most isolated trails.

After Kokee Lodge, the drive rises and curves another 1.5 miles until it reaches Kalalau Valley Lookout, an awe-inspiring view over the beautiful, isolated valley at the end of the Na Pali Coast Trail. High rock spires, sheer green cliffs, and distant waterfalls combine to form a landscape of incredible beauty. An inspired viewer once commented that if there was a Garden of Eden, it must have looked like Kalalau. At one time the site of a thriving Hawaiian community, the valley is unoccupied now. For a period in the early 1970s, the valley hosted a resident hippie population, living off the land and growing their blessed weed. A state crackdown finally forced them out. Today the valley is deserted, except for backpackers making the 11-mile trek along the coastal cliffs, and access is strictly controlled.

In 1892, the valley was the scene of a tragedy peculiar to the Hawaiian Islands. A small band of lepers, led by a man named Koolau, sought refuge

View of Kalalau Valley from Kalalau Lookout in Kokee Park.

in the far reaches of the valley. At that time persons afflicted with the disease were sent to the infamous leper colony at Kalaupapa on Molokai, where more perished from hunger, abuse, and neglect than from the disease itself. Koolau and his followers were pursued by police and soldiers until all were killed or captured except Koolau himself. With the aid of his wife, who did not have the disease, and who kept him supplied by making hazardous trips down the face of the cliffs, Koolau successfully eluded capture until his death two years later. When the author Jack London visited Hawaii in 1915, he was so moved by the incident that he used it as the basis for his short story, "Koolau the Leper."

From the Kalalau Lookout, the road continues relatively straight and flat again for 0.5 mile, until it ends at Puu o Kila, another lookout over Kalalau Valley. From here, on a clear day it is possible to see the summit of Mount Waialeale, although it is difficult to identify. The peak is relatively flat and not especially prominent. Also, as one of the world's wettest spots, it is usually covered by clouds. Although the pavement ends at Puu O Kila, a rough jeep road continues until it also ends at the Pihea Trail. This road is all that remains of an abandoned plan to build a connecting route across Kauai's pristine Na Pali wilderness between Kokee and Hanalei on Kauai's north shore. Fortunately, conservation and ecological interests prevailed, and the road will probably never be built.

The Pihea Trail is the north entrance to the Alakai Swamp. Covering more than 10 square miles, this upland swamp is the largest in the islands. Because it has remained almost untouched by man, it provides a refuge for some of Hawaii's most endangered birds and plants, some of which exist nowhere else in the world. The Alakai swamp, acting much like a giant sponge soaking up rainfall, feeds dozens of streams and waterfalls throughout Kauai. A brief foray into the swamp here is a marvelous introduction to a world of watery weirdness. A boardwalk is under construction, and, although progress is slow, it may have reached Pihea by the time this book appears. But boardwalk or not, it is essential to remain on the trail. People have disappeared in this boggy wilderness.

MOLOKAI

Molokai is the fifth largest of the Hawaiian Islands and is between 1.3 and 1.8 million years old. Formed by two volcanoes, it was once part of the island of Maui. When seen from Oahu, Molokai appears to be two separate islands—a relatively flat one to the west and a mountainous one to the east. And, in fact, these two regions are very different from each other. The east is dry, cut by eroded gullies, and even has an area called "The Desert Strip." The west is lush and well watered, with wide, fertile amphitheater valleys, rain forests, and montagne bogs.

More than half of Molokai's population is Hawaiian, a larger proportion than any other island, and the pace of life is slow. There are no traffic lights, no movie theaters, few restaurants, and no night life. That keeps some tourists away and attracts others.

Molokai once had a flourishing pineapple industry. When the plantation closed in 1982, the island lost its main employer, and the economy has never recovered. An attempt to replace pineapple with tourism failed (six hotels were planned on the east end beaches) when the tourists did not come. Only one hotel was built and it suffers from low occupancy. The unemployment and welfare rates on the island remain high. Molokai Ranch, the major land owner, has embarked upon an ambitious plan to rejuvenate the economy (see below), but only time will tell if this plan will succeed.

For many years Molokai was known primarily for the leper colony on remote Kalaupapa Peninsula, where victims of the disease were once confined. With the discovery of medication that arrests the illness, the remaining patients at the settlement are free to leave if they wish. Kalaupapa is now a National Historic Park and can be visited (see below).

For tourists willing to go off the beaten path, Molokai provides a rewarding scenic experience.

Area: 261 square miles
Population: 6,700
Airports: Main: Hoolehua.
Secondary: Kalaupapa.
Rental car offices: Airport.

15

Molokai: The Last Hawaiian Place

General description: This 60-mile drive begins at the Kalua Koi Hotel on Molokai's western end, traverses the dry western third of the island, and veers north for a spectacular view of the isolated coastline. Turning south, the route then follows the southern shore of lush east Molokai to the road's end at Halawa Valley. Five county beach parks lie along the drive.

Special attractions: Papohaku Beach, African Wildlife Park, Kalaupapa Overlook, Phallic Rock, Kapuaiwa Coconut Grove, Halawa Valley, ancient fishponds, hiking, camping, swimming, snorkeling, scuba diving, fishing.

Location: The island of Molokai.

Drive route numbers: Kalua Koi Road, Hawaii Highways 460 (Maunaloa Highway), 470 (Kalae Highway), and 450 (Kamehameha V Highway).

Camping: There are five campgrounds on the route: Kiowea Beach Park, Palaau State Park, Papohaku Beach and Onealii Beach County Parks, and Waialua Congregational Church. Permits are required.

Services: Kalua Koi Hotel: accommodations, restaurant, bar. Kaunakakai: 2 small hotels, restaurants, gas, and limited shopping. Kualapuu: restaurant, gas. There are no services elsewhere along the route.

Nearby attractions: Kawakiu Bay, Kalaupapa National Historic Park, Kamakou Forest Reserve, Sandalwood Pit, Waikolu Valley Overlook, Iliiliopae Heiau, Moaula and Hipuapua Waterfalls.

 The Drive

Leaving the hotel, the drive proceeds south along Kalua Koi Road and passes through a large real estate development offering lots of 5 acres or more, some of them fronting Papohaku Beach (one of the longest and widest white sand beaches in the islands). First offered to the public in the early 1980s, sales in this isolated *kiawe*/grassland landscape have been slow, and home construction has been even slower. Access to Papohaku Beach is through several public right of ways in the development and via Papohaku Beach County Park, a shaded, green oasis where camping is permitted. Strong offshore currents and a heavy shore break often make swimming unsafe, but Papohaku Beach is a beautiful place for a stroll.

Reversing direction, the drive returns toward the hotel and continues east on Kalua Koi Road. Off to the right, but not visible from the road, is the Molokai Ranch African Wildlife Park, which offers safari tours of a re-creation of an African savanna. Over a thousand animals roam freely within its 400 acres, including Barbary sheep, oryx, and giraffes. A visit to the park must be arranged in advance at the Kalua Koi Hotel.

Kalua Koi Road reaches a junction with HI 460 4.5 miles from the hotel, where a right turn leads to the small former plantation town of Maunaloa (population 650). Molokai Ranch owns virtually all of the land in the town and much of West Molokai, and has embarked upon a long-range redevelopment plan, which envisions additional housing, a newly created town square, a small hotel, and even a movie theater—something Molokai does not have. Reaction by residents has been mixed. Opponents are mainly those whose old, run-down homes, rented to them by the ranch, are due to be demolished. As of this writing, the town offers a colorful store boasting a kite factory and oriental knick-knacks, a gas station, and a small restaurant.

The drive continues eastward on HI 460; gradually it leaves the dry pasture land for more fertile and watered soil where seed corn and coffee are grown. Twelve miles from Maunaloa turn north onto HI 470 toward the town of Kualapuu, headquarters of the largest coffee plantation on Molokai. A visitor center offers displays, a free tasting room, and coffee and related products for sale.

HI 470 continues north for about 4 miles and ends at Palaau State Park. There is a wooded campground here. From the parking lot it is a short walk to Kalaupapa Lookout for a dramatic view of Kalaupapa Peninsula and Molokai's isolated north shore. Site of the Hansen's Disease (leprosy) settlement made famous by the Belgian priest Father Damien, Kalaupapa is now a National Historic Park. Before Damien's time, persons with leprosy were transported to the settlement and left to fend for themselves—sometimes they were forced to swim ashore by boat captains who refused to put in at the colony. Only sixty-nine patients remain in residence as of the date of this writing, and they do so voluntarily; they are free to leave if they wish.

You can visit the settlement with advance permission. A fee is charged for a tour; it includes a bus ride through the town, a visit to Father Damien's church, and a stop at Kalawao Park for an incomparable view of Molokai's sea cliffs, the highest in the world.

There are three ways to reach the settlement. A 2-mile trail leads down the cliff from Palaau State Park; you can descend by foot or by mule. The mule ride has been an on-and-off affair. After operating for years, it closed down in 1993. It started up again in 1995, and as of the date of publication, it was still running. The third way to reach the settlement is by air. Molokai Air Shuttle and Island Air offer daily flights from Honolulu and from Molokai Airport.

Molokai: The Last Hawaiian Place

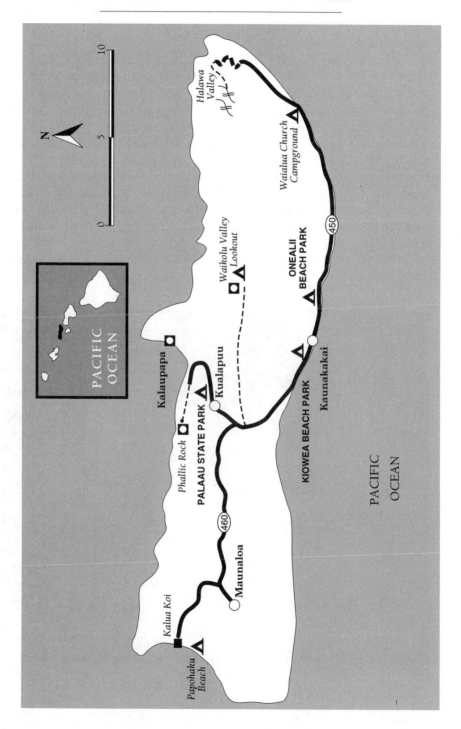

Another trail from the lookout leads into the woods along the ridgeline to Phallic Rock, a large, explicitly realistic fertility symbol. According to legend, in ancient times Hawaiian women came to the site to pray for offspring and safe childbirth.

The drive now retraces HI 470 back to the intersection with HI 460 and continues south. For those with four-wheel-drive vehicles, a 20-mile round-trip side excursion is possible to Kamakou Forest Preserve, via Maunahui Road. A sandalwood boat lies along this route, which is actually a pit shaped like a ship's hold that was used to measure a shipload of the wood during the days of the sandalwood trade. The demand from China for this fragrant wood became so great, and so profitable for Hawaiian chiefs, that in a period of twenty years virtually all the sandalwood was stripped from Hawaiian forests. In the process, many of the chiefs forced commoners to work seven days a week, cutting and hauling the wood, with no time to tend to their own fields, causing neglect of their crops and widespread starvation.

The practical part of this side trip, even for four-wheel-drive vehicles,

Phallic Rock.

ends at Waikolu Lookout. Here, a dramatic view of Waikolu Valley unfolds, from its headwall all the way to the ocean. A small picnic area and a campground are across from the lookout. More daring (and skilled) drivers may continue to Pepeopae, for a boardwalked stroll through an incomparable native forest, and one of the few accessible montagne bogs in Hawaii. It ends at another spectacular lookout, this one over Pelekunu Valley. But the road is narrow, very rough, and almost always muddy.

The main part of the scenic drive now reaches the south coast, about 2.5 miles from Maunahui Road. Just past the Kapuaiwa Coconut Grove is Kiowea Beach Park, a palm-lined campground under jurisdiction of Hawaiian Home Lands. The route proceeds straight through Kaunakakai (population 2,400), the only town of any size on the island. On the other side (east) of town, the route becomes HI 450. Three miles beyond the town, a spacious, oceanfront campground at Onealii Beach County Park provides restrooms, showers, drinking water, and a large pavilion.

For the remainder of the trip the drive follows the coast, with the mountainous spine of Molokai on the left and the sea on the right. Across the Kalohi Channel, the island of Lanai is clearly visible for most of the way. Much of the south shore consists of mud flats, extending up 0.5 mile off shore and formed by thousands of years of runoff from the mountains. Ancient fishponds line the coast. Used to trap ocean fish, and keep them alive

View of Molokai's north coast from Kalawao on Kalaupapa.

until used, the ponds were owned exclusively by the chiefs in old Hawaii. More of these ponds have survived on this coastline than in any similar location in the islands.

As the drive turns slightly northeast, the mud flats give way to rocky shoreline, small bays, and pocket sandy beaches. Modest settlements appear, usually no more than one or two houses, as the drive rounds curves and bays. The island of Maui soon comes into view to the southeast.

The remains of the Iliiliopae Heiau, one of the largest in the islands, lie off the highway about 14 miles past Kaunakakai and a mile east of the Lady of Seven Sorrows Church. You find the *heiau* by parking near a small bridge with white pipe railings. At mailbox 234, a narrow dirt road leads toward the mountains. If the gate is closed, there is small trail. However, this is private property, and the owner's rights must be respected. The *heiau* is at the end of this dirt road on the left side. Nothing but the massive rock platform remains, but it provides mute evidence of its once impressive size. Iliiliopae was a *luakini heiau*, a temple where human sacrifices were offered.

Continuing on HI 450, the picnic grounds of the Waialua Congregational Church provide a lovely, exclusive-use campground, on a scenic shoreline. A user fee is charged. The route now begins to climb, leaving the coast, and winding through forests and lush pasture land. It then makes a steep, curved, mile-long descent into Halawa Valley, the only one of Molokai's north-

Church in Halawa Valley.

ern coast amphitheater valleys accessible by vehicle. The road ends at a small beach park. Two sandy beaches are on each side of the bay, and two beautiful waterfalls, Moalua and Hipuapua, lie a short distance up the valley. Moalua is accessible by a 2-mile trail.

Halawa Valley was a prosperous farming community until two devastating *tsunami* struck in 1946 and 1960. Now only a few families live in the valley. As of this writing, public access to the two waterfalls was being disputed by valley residents who claim that the trail crosses private land, which could make the owners liable for hikers's injuries. Check with local authorities for information on public access.

LANAI

Lanai is the sixth largest of the Hawaiian Islands. Formed by a single shield volcano, it is between 1.3 and 1.8 million years old. It was once part of the island of Maui and is now part of Maui County. Lanai is one of the two main Hawaiian Islands that is privately owned (the other is Niihau, forbidden to visitors). In ancient times, Lanai was a feared and forbidden place. For centuries, Hawaiians considered it a place of evil spirits, and it remained uninhabited. It was only after a high Maui chief banished his wayward son to the island and he later returned unscathed that Hawaiians began to populate it.

For years, Lanai was the world's largest pineapple plantation. The plantation closed in 1992 and since then the island has been struggling to redefine itself as a tourist destination. The Dole Company, which owns more than ninety-eight percent of the island, has built two luxury hotels with golf courses, and has retrained much of the agricultural work force to handle hotel positions. So far, occupancy rates have only been fair.

For the tourist who is satisfied with golf and beaches, a paved road connects the two hotels and the island's best beach. But to take advantage of Lanai's scenic drives, a four-wheel-drive vehicle is necessary. Lanai's attractions are more rugged than those on the other islands and harder to get to. However, those willing to make the effort will find the attractions equally rewarding.

Area: 140 square miles
Population: 2,400
Airport: Lanai City
Rental car offices: Lanai City

16

Kaunolu Village Site, Luahiwa Petroglyphs, and Hulopoe Beach

General description: This 34-mile loop descends from Lanai City to the island's only commercial harbor, explores an important ancient Hawaiian village site, stops at the prettiest beach on Lanai, and visits a significant petroglyph field.

Special attractions: Kaumalapau Harbor, Kaunolu Village archaeological site, Hulopoe Beach, Manele Bay, Luahiwa petroglyphs, hiking, camping, swimming, snorkeling, scuba diving.

Location: Southeastern section of the island of Lanai.

Drive route numbers: Hawaii Highway 440, Kaupili Road, Kaunolu Trail (requires four-wheel-drive).

Camping: A campground is located at Hulopoe Beach, permit required.

Services: Lanai City: the Lodge at Koele and the Hotel Lanai (10 rooms) are the only accommodations; they also have restaurants and bars. Gas, limited food service, and very limited shopping are available in the town. Hulopoe Beach: accommodations, restaurant, and bar at the Manele Bay Hotel. There are no services elsewhere along the route.

Nearby attractions: Garden of the Gods, Shipwreck Beach, Polihua Beach (see Scenic Drive 18).

 The Drive

A four-wheel-drive vehicle is required for the Kaunolu Village portion of this drive, which will also serve for Scenic Drives 17 and 18. Rentals are available in Lanai City. As signs to the Luahiwa petroglyphs are sometimes knocked down, it is advisable to ask directions at one of the hotels before starting out on the drive. Beginning in Lanai City (population 2,100), the route proceeds 7 miles southeast on Hawaii Highway 440 (HI 440) to Kaumalapau, the island's only harbor. Lanai was once the world's largest pineapple plantation, and the harbor was busy with barges taking the fruit to market. Today, the plantation is gone, and traffic has been reduced to one general cargo barge per week. Much of the equipment on the pier is no longer in use, and only one tug is sometimes moored in the harbor. An occasional pleasure boat may seek shelter behind its protective breakwater, and scuba divers use the edge of the harbor to make a deep "wall dive."

From the harbor, the drive returns the way it came, along the highway for 3.3 miles, turning right on unmarked Kaupili Road. This dirt road passes through rows of former pineapple fields. The rust-colored road and fields attest to the ferrous oxide in the soil, which formed as the iron-laden lava flows that created the island deteriorated. In 2.2 miles the route turns right again and after 0.5 mile, jogs left and then right (watch for signs to Kaunolu) on what soon becomes a very steep, rocky, jeep road. Four-wheel-drive and low transfer case need to be engaged for this precipitous descent, which is not dangerous if taken slowly and carefully.

The road ends at the sea at Kaunolu, the scenic site of an ancient fishing village. Said to be a favorite vacationing spot for Kamehameha, the first king of all the Hawaiian Islands, the remains of his residence can still be seen. The village was surveyed by the Bishop Museum in 1921 and 1991, and museum archaeologists excavated much of the site in 1993. Today, the village is a National Historic Landmark, and a path runs through the area with signs identifying what remains of the more important locations. These include house sites, watch tower, fishing shrine, *heiau*, and a canoe shed. Kaunolu was once Lanai's major settlement, with over 2,000 inhabitants, which about equals the present day population of the entire island.

An opening in the cliff wall on the west side of the village is known as Kahekili's Leap, named for a Maui chief famed for daring feats. He particularly enjoyed *lele kawa*, or cliff jumping, and "leaps" bearing his name are found on other islands. At Kaunolu, he would spring from the vertigo-inducing precipice, narrowly missing a ledge which jutted out be-

Rocky shore at Kaunolu.

Kaunolu Village Site,
Luahiwa Petroglyphs, and Hulopoe Beach

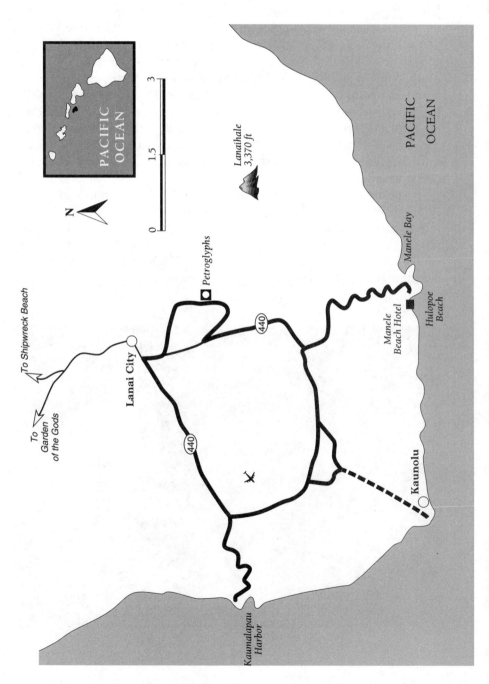

low, and plunge into the sea, challenging other chiefs to follow him. It is also said that Kamehameha punished minor offenders by requiring that they make the leap.

Leaving Kaunolu, the drive then backtracks on Kaunolu Trail and rejoins Kaupili Road. A right turn on Kaupili Road continues the tour through the abandoned pineapple fields. After 5 miles Kaupili Road intersects HI 440 and the drive turns right, following HI 440 as it descends to Hulopoe and Manele Bays. Hulopoe, a beautiful crescent of white sand on Lanai's south shore, is shared by the luxurious Manele Bay Hotel; Hulopoe is the only campground on the island. Another ancient fishing village existed between Manele and Hulopoe, and some of its ruins are still visible. Hulopoe is part of a marine life conservation district, and on the east side of the bay a lava shelf contains colorful coral formations. Unfortunately, Hurricane Iniki damaged these formations in 1992. Swimming, snorkeling, and scuba diving are all good in the vicinity.

The drive again retraces part of the route, proceeding north on HI 440. At 2.2 miles past the junction of the highway and Kaupili Road, the drive turns right on unmarked Hoike Road, which angles back sharply. In about a mile, a dirt road crosses, and the drive turns left on this road, proceeding another 0.5 mile to the Luahiwa petroglyphs. Signs usually show the way, but they are sometimes removed by persons who wish to preserve the carv-

Large rock at Luahiwa petroglyph site.

ings from accidental or deliberate damage by visitors.

Luahiwa was once the site of a *heiau* dedicated to the rain gods *Ku* and *Hina* that was built in a cluster of boulders. The *heiau* is gone but the boulders remain and offer fine examples of ancient Hawaiian rock carvings. Most are of human figures, but dogs and horses are also shown. Some of the carvings date to before 1600, although most were made between the eighteenth and nineteenth centuries. Unfortunately, some of the older figures have been altered by later carvers, destroying their original meaning; others have been defaced by modern graffiti. The largest rock in the field contains over 135 petroglyphs.

From Luahiwa, the drive returns to HI 440 and Lanai City.

17

The Roof of the Island
to Keomuku Beach

General description: This 30-mile loop begins in Lanai City, and traverses most of the Munro Trail, a jeep road leading along a forested ridge to Lanaihale, the highest point on the island. It then descends a steep trail to the eastern shore, exploring abandoned villages and small, isolated beaches before connecting with HI 430 to return to Lanai City.
Special attractions: Munro Trail, Lanaihale, hiking, swimming, snorkeling, beachcombing.
Location: The eastern side of Lanai Island.
Drive route numbers: Munro Trail, Awehi Trail, Hawaii Highway 430 (Keomuku Road).
Camping: There are no campgrounds along the drive.
Services: Lanai City: the Lodge at Koele and the Hotel Lanai (10 rooms) are the only accommodations, and they also have restaurants and bars. Gas, limited food service, and very limited shopping are available in the town. There are no services elsewhere along the route.
Nearby attractions: Shipwreck Beach (see Scenic Drive 18).

 The Drive

A four-wheel-drive vehicle is required for this trip. Weather can sometimes be a problem on this drive. Clouds tend to form along the Munro Trail ridge, especially in the afternoon. Rainy weather, when it arrives, can last for days. This drive should not be attempted in such conditions. Mist and rain will restrict visibility, and parts of the trail can become muddy and impassable. The Awehi Trail may become flooded and dangerous during and after rain storms. Even the coastal part of the trip should not be made in wet weather. Despite its level grade, four-wheel-drive vehicles can get mired down in the mucky pools that form along the dirt road and can remain for days after the last rain. It is a good idea to check with the hotel or other local authorities before setting out.

To reach the Munro Trail, the route proceeds 1.25 miles past the Koele Lodge on Keomuku Road (HI 430) and turns right onto a tree-lined paved road to a sign for the start of the trail. This upland portion of the island was reforested in the early 1900s by naturalist and Lanai Ranch manager George

The Roof of the Island to Keomuku Beach

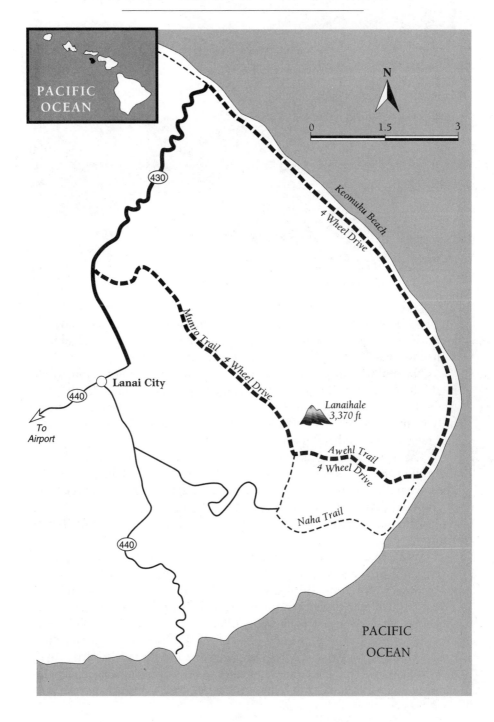

Jeep on the Munro Trail, with the island of Molokai in the distance.

Munro. He planted thousands of eucalyptus, ironwoods, Norfolk Island pine, and other trees in an attempt to restore Lanai's watershed, which had been ruined by years of goat, sheep, and cattle grazing.

The trail first crosses a meadow and several small gullies before reaching Maunalei Gulch, the scene of a massacre of Lanaians in 1778, during a war with the island of Hawaii. Some people believe that the island has never fully recovered from this event, which nearly exterminated the population and ravaged the land and its crops.

The drive then begins to climb steadily, but once on the the ridgeline the route levels out a bit until it reaches Lanaihale (3,370 feet), about 5.5 miles from the beginning of the trail. On a clear day, five of the main islands of the Hawaiian chain may be seen from here: Molokai, Maui, Hawaii, Kahoolawe, and Oahu. Only Kauai and Niihau are absent from the family group.

A little over a mile past the summit, the drive turns sharply left on the Awehi Trail. It is a steep, rugged descent, requiring low transfer case and low gear, as well as four-wheel-drive. It reaches the coast in about 3 miles— a long 3 miles. The drive then turns left on a dirt road running parallel to the coast. Turnouts to narrow beaches offer views of Maui and Molokai and provide secluded swimming and beachcombing. Three miles after reaching the coast, the drive passes Club Lanai, a destination for tourists arriving by boat from Maui. Club Lanai does not cater to visitors from Lanai, except for an all-you-can-eat-and-drink buffet lunch.

Two miles farther up the coast the deserted village of Keomuku is marked by a small abandoned church. It is difficult to believe, but two attempts to grow sugar were made in this dry, desolate place. In 1802 a lone Chinese man, Wong Tze Chun, built a small mill and began to grow cane. The project was not successful, Chun disassembled the mill, and he and his machinery moved away to parts unknown.

It was not until 1895 that another attempt was made, this time on a much larger scale when a plantation was established. It too failed when a plague struck the workers, and when water needed for irrigation turned brackish. Local legend claims that these calamities occurred because the plantation destroyed a *heiau* and used its rocks for a railway bed. Exploring off the road in the *kiawe* thickets can reveal many relics of the village—house sites, machinery, and even a small locomotive—almost overgrown by a tangle of vegetation.

The drive continues to follow the coast through a forest of *kiawe* and ironwood trees for another 5 miles, until it joins HI 430 and turns left for the 9-mile, winding ascent to Lanai City.

18

Garden of the Gods,
Polihua, and Shipwreck Beach

General description: This 29-mile, four-wheel-drive loop crosses former pineapple fields, visits an area of interesting rock formations, and follows the entire length of two of Hawaii's most isolated beaches.
Special attractions: Garden of the Gods, Polihua Beach, Shipwreck Beach, hiking, fishing, beachcombing.
Location: The northern end of the island of Lanai.
Drive route numbers: Polihua Road, Polihua Trail, Shipwreck Beach Trail, Hawaii Highway 430 (Keomuko Road).
Camping: There are no campgrounds on the route.
Services: Lanai City: accommodations, restaurants and bars are available at the Lodge at Koele and the Hotel Lanai. Gas, limited food, and shopping can be found in town. There are no services elsewhere along the drive.
Nearby attractions: Kaumalapau Harbor, Kaunolu Village, Hulopoe Beach, Luahiwa petroglyphs (see Scenic Drive 16).

 The Drive

Although a conventional car can manage the first part of this drive to the Garden of the Gods, a four-wheel-drive vehicle is essential for the remainder of the trip. **IMPORTANT NOTE:** Shifting sands and beach erosion may obliterate the jeep track past Polihua Beach, making it impossible to do this drive as a loop. Another problem might be encountered at the south end of Shipwreck Beach, where the road is sometimes blocked at the abandoned Federal Camp. Check locally for the latest information. If either of these situations arise, the drive can be done in two increments—the first to Polihua via Garden of the Gods, and the second to Shipwreck Beach via HI 430.

Beginning in Lanai City, on HI 430 (Keomuku Road), the drive turns to the left just past Koele Lodge, between the Lodge's stables and tennis courts. This is Polihua Road, a dirt road, but in good condition. The route turns right at the first crossroad and stays left at forks from then on. Passing through an ironwood forest, the route continues for 5 miles and reaches the Garden of the Gods, a pretentious title for an area of eroded rock and soil

Garden of the Gods, Polihua, and Shipwreck Beach

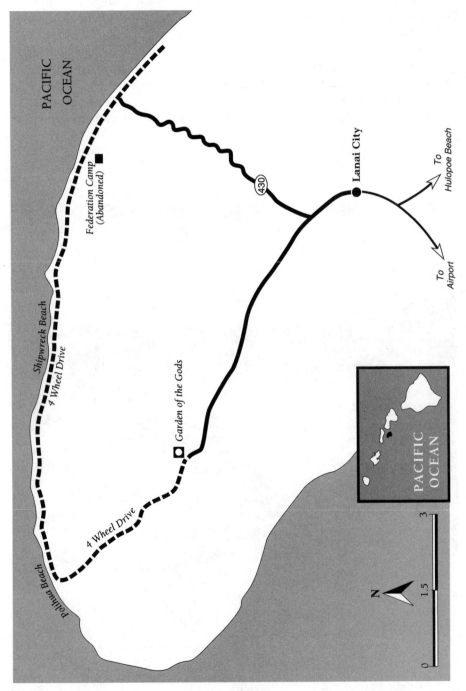

enhanced by numerous rock cairns added by visitors over the years.

The drive then goes straight through the rock formations, bearing right at a fork. The road quickly deteriorates to a rough, four-wheel-drive track, which descends steeply for 4 miles to Polihua Beach. About 0.75 mile from the Garden of the Gods, a fork to the left leads to Kaena Point, the site of a former penal colony for women. Established in 1830 as a place of exile for women convicted of adultery, a similar colony was founded for men on Kahoolawe. The men, more adventurous than the women, soon began raiding Maui coastal villages, and according to one story, paddled to Lanai and persuaded most of the convict women to go off with them. True or not, the authorities closed both colonies in 1843 and returned the occupants to their homes.

Grounded ship offshore and wreck on shoreline, Shipwreck Beach.

Polihua, a long, white sand beach, secluded from the rest of the island, is almost always deserted. A strong offshore current, sometimes exerting the force of a fast-flowing river, makes swimming dangerous, but it is a wild, beautiful spot. At the shoreline, the drive turns west and follows the coast along the entire length of Shipwreck Beach, 10 miles of narrow track and shifting sands. (As explained previously, if the track is difficult to find, covered with soft sand, or obliterated by wave action, continuation of the drive should not be attempted. Even four-wheel-drive vehicles can become stuck under these conditions, and help is far away.)

GLOSSARY

Most of the Hawaiian words in this glossary are found in this book. Others may be encountered while scenic driving on the islands. Understanding them will enhance your trip experience. It does not include commonly recognized words such as aloha, lei, or luau.

a'a - one of the two types of lava flows, a'a has a rough, clinker-like appearance.

ahu - stone cairn, usually used to mark a route or a trail

aina - land, earth.

alaloa - highway, main road, usually around the coastal circumference of an island. Sometimes called the "King's Highway."

ali'i - chief, noble, member of the ruling class in old Hawaii and during the kingdom.

hale - house, structure.

haole - originally a foreigner, now a Caucasian, whether foreign or not.

hapuu - a native Hawaiian tree fern.

heiau - a temple or place of worship of the old Hawaiian religion. Nothing remains of most heiau today except their stone foundations.

holua - an ancient Hawaiian slide and the sled used on it.

iki - little, such as Kilauea-Iki (Little Kilauea).

kahuna - priest, expert.

kai - sea, sea water.

kamaaina - accurately, a person born in Hawaii, but sometimes used to denote a longtime resident.

Kamehameha - A chief of a district of the island of Hawaii, who, by conquest, became the first king of all the Hawaiian Islands. Born around 1758, he ruled until his death in 1819. The next four successors to the crown also took the title "Kamehameha" and for that reason he is also referred to as Kamehameha I.

kapu - taboo, forbidden. When seen on a sign, it means keep out, or do not touch.

kiawe - a drought-resistant tree, closely related to mesquite, used extensively throughout Hawaii to reforest dry, leeward areas.

King's Highway - old Hawaiian road or trail, usually around the outer circumference of an island (see alaloa).

kona - leeward, particularly the leeward side of an island. Kona winds blow toward the leeward side, as opposed to the customary trade winds, which blow toward the windward side of the islands.

koolau - windward, the windward side of an island.

local - obviously not a Hawaiian word, but it has a specialized meaning in the islands. A "local" person in Hawaii is not simply a resident. "Local" has ethnic connotations, referring to persons of mixed race, usually of a Polynesian/Oriental background. It is not pejorative or insulting.

makai - toward the ocean. In Hawaii, directions are sometimes given in relation to a geographic reference. Persons asking directions may be told to go "makai three blocks, then go Diamond Head two more blocks."

mauka - toward the mountains (see makai above).

mauna - mountain, as in Mauna Kea (white mountain).

moana - ocean.

ohia - the most common native tree in Hawaii, thousands of acres of ohia forest still exist, particularly on the island of Hawaii. Ohia grows at elevations from 1,000 to 9,000 feet, and depending on growing conditions, can appear as anything from a bush to a forest giant. It and the hapuu are among the first plants to regenerate on new lava fields.

pahoehoe - one of the two kinds of lava flows, pahoehoe has a smooth surface when unbroken.

pali - cliff, precipice.

Pele - goddess of fire and of the volcano.

petroglyphs - obviously not a Hawaiian word, but used to describe ancient rock carvings found in selected places on all of the inhabited Hawaiian Islands. The purpose and meaning of petroglyphs and their creators are unknown.

pu'u - hill, rise.

wai - fresh water, liquid.

APPENDIX
Sources of More Information
For additional information about the scenic drives
please contact the following agencies and organizations.

Drive 1

County Department of Parks
650 S. King Street
Honolulu, HI 96813
808-523-4525

Sea Life Park
41-202 Kalanianaole Hwy
Waimanalo, HI 96795
808-259-7933

Drive 2

County Department of Parks
650 S. King Street
Honolulu, HI 96813
808-523-4525

Division of State Parks
P.O. Box 621
Honolulu, HI 96809
808-587-0300

Hoomaluhia Botanical Garden
45-680 Luluku Road
Kaneohe, HI 96744
808-235-6636

Polynesian Cultural Center
55-370 Kamehameha Highway
Laie, HI 96762
808-293-3333

Drive 3

Camp Erdman
Central Branch YMCA, Camp Office
401 Atkinson Drive
Honolulu, HI 96814
808-941-3344

Camp Mokuleia
68-729 Farrington Highway
Waialua, HI 96791
808-637-6241

County Department of Parks
650 S. King Street
Honolulu, HI 96813
808-523-4525

Drive 4

County Department of Parks
War Memorial Center
Wailuku, HI 96793
808-243-7389

Haleakala National Park
PO Box 369
Makawao, HI 96768
808-572-9306

Drive 5

County Department of Parks
War Memorial Center
Wailuku, HI 96793
808-243-7389

Division of State Parks
P.O. Box 1049
Wailuku, HI 96793
808-984-8109

Hana Kai Resort
808-248-8426

Heavenly Hana Inn
808-248-8442

Hotel Hana Maui
808-248-8211

Drive 6

Camp Pecusa
800 Olowalu Village
Lahaina, HI 96761
808-661-4303

County Department of Parks
War Memorial Center
Wailuku, HI 96793
808-243-7389

Maui Land and Pineapple Company
Honolua Division, (Camping
Permits)
Lahaina, HI 96761
808-669-6201

Drive 7

County Department of Parks
25 Aupuni Street
Hilo, HI 96720
808-961-8311

Division of State Parks
P.O. Box 936
Hilo, HI 96720
808-933-4200

Kalani Honua Conference and
Retreat Center
RR2, Box 4500
Kalapana, HI 96778
808-965-7828

Drive 8

Hawaii Volcanoes National Park
Volcano, HI 96718
808-967-7184

Kilauea Military Camp
Hawaii Volcanoes National Park
Volcano, HI 96718
808-967-8333

Volcano House Hotel
P.O. Box 53
Volcano, HI 96718
808-967-7321

Drive 9

County Department of Parks
25 Aupuni Street
Hilo, HI 96720
808-961-8311

Division of State Parks
P.O. Box 936
Hilo, HI 96720
808-933-4200

Onizuka Center for International
Astronomy
808-961-2180

Drive 10

County Department of Parks
25 Aupuni Street
Hilo, HI 96720
808-961-8311

Drive 11

County Department of Parks
25 Aupuni Street
Hilo, HI 96720
808-961-8311

Division of State Parks
P.O. Box 936
Hilo HI 96720
808-933-4200

Drive 12

County Department of Parks
4280A Rice Street
Lihue, HI 96766
808-241-6660

Division of State Parks
3060 Eiwa Street
Lihue, HI 96766
808-241-3444

Kauai YMCA Camp Naue
PO Box 1786
Lihue, HI 96766
808-246-9090

Drive 13

County Department of Parks
4280A Rice Street
Lihue, HI 96766
808-241-6660

Division of State Parks
3060 Eiwa Street
Lihue, HI 96766
808-241-3444

Drive 14

County Department of Parks
4280A Rice Street
Lihue, HI 96766
808-241-6660

Division of State Parks
3060 Eiwa Street
Lihue, HI 96766
808-241-3444

Kokee Lodge
P. O. Box 819
Waimea, HI 96796
808-335-6061

Drive 15

County Department of Parks
P, O. Box 526
Kaunakakai, HI 96748
808-553-3204

Division of State Parks
P. O. Box 1049
Wailuku, HI 96793
808-984-8109
(Office is on Maui.)

Hawaiian Home Lands
P. O. Box 198
Hoolehua, HI 96729
808-567-6104

Waialua Congregational Church
Jo-Ann K. Simms, Caretaker
Star Route 335
Molokai, HI 96748
808-558-8150\8268

Drive 16

The Lanai Company
P. O. Box 310
Lanai City, HI 96763
Attn: Camping Permits
808-565-8206

Drive 17

The Lanai Company
P. O. Box 310
Lanai City, HI 96763
808-565-8206

Drive 18

The Lanai Company
P. O. Box 310
Lanai City, HI 96763
808-565-8206

INDEX

133

ABOUT THE AUTHOR

Richard McMahon has been a part time freelance writer for more than thirty years. His book, *Camping Hawaii* (University of Hawaii Press), was published in 1994, and *Adventuring In Hawaii* (Sierra Club Books), was published in 1996.

He holds M.A. degrees in English (Writing) and in history from the University of Hawaii.

Falcon Press Publishing has **FALCON** GUIDES to hiking, mountain biking, rock climbing, walking, scenic driving, fishing, rockhounding, paddling, birding, wildlife viewing, and camping. Here are a few titles currently available, but this list grows every year. If you would like a free catalog with an undated list of available titles, call FALCON at the toll-free number at the bottom of this page.

HIKING GUIDES:

State-specific guides to Alaska, Alberta, Arizona, California, Colorado, Georgia, Florida, Idaho, Maine, Michigan, Minnesota, Montana, Nevada, New Hampshire, New Mexico, New York, North Carolina, Oregon, Southern New England, Tennessee, Texas, Utah, Vermont, Virginia, Washington, and Wyoming. Regional guides to Northern Arizona, Southern Arizona, and Hot Springs of the Pacific Northwest.

MOUNTAIN BIKING GUIDES:

Arizona, Colorado, New York, Northern New England, New Mexico, Southern New England, and Utah. Local mountain biking guides to Bozeman, Colorado Springs, Denver-Boulder, and Moab.

ROCK CLIMBING GUIDES:

Colorado, Montana, New Mexico/Texas, and Utah.

PADDLING:

Colorado, Missouri, Montana, and Oregon

BIRDING GUIDES:

Arizona, Minnesota, and Montana.

WILDLIFE VIEWING GUIDES:

Alaska, Arizona, California, Colorado, Florida, Idaho, Indiana, Iowa, Kentucky, Massachusetts, Montana, Nebraska, Nevada, New Hampshire, New Mexico, North Carolina, North Dakota, Ohio, Oregon, Tennessee, Texas, Utah, Vermont, Virginia, Washington, and Wisconsin.

FISHING:

Alaska, Beartooths, Maine, Michigan, and Montana.

SCENIC DRIVING:

Alaska/Yukon, Arizona, Beartooth Highway, California, Colorado, Georgia, Hawaii, Michigan, Minnesota, Montana, New England, New Mexico, Oregon, Ozarks, Texas, Utah, Washington and Wisconsin. Plus, National Forest Scenic Byways, National Forest Scenic Byways II, and Back Country Byways. Historic trail driving guides to the Oregon Trail, Lewis and Clark Trail, and the Pony Express Trail.

■ *To order any of these books, check with your local bookseller or call FALCON at* 1-800-582-2665

FALCON™